THE
VOCABULARY
WORKBOOK
FOR 6TH GRADE

RASTIC TANGIBLE ARID
OBLIVIOUS CONGRUENT approac
SWARM hypothesis IMMIGR
ARD GENUINE suspense GIGANT
RHYTHM
IRRIGATE procce GIST
HRONOLOGICAL ORIGIN hero
QUEST UNRULY QUOTE
squeeze SCARCE ferociou
ARTIFACT unanimous
XTEND CEASE KNACK
MPLE NARRATE DECL
VERDICT EXAGGERATE NUI

Dedicated to all the readers and writers, with the hope that their mastery of language skills will bring about better understanding and peaceful dialogue between future generations of our world.

Interior and Cover Designer: Angie Chiu
Art Producer: Tom Hood
Editor: Michael Goodman

ISBN: Print 978-1-64611-468-9

R0

THE
VOCABULARY WORKBOOK

FOR

6TH GRADE

Weekly Activities to
Boost Your Word Power

KELLY ANNE McLE

ROC

CONTENTS

INTRODUCTION

I have been a passionate writer my entire life and a teacher of writing for the past eight years. Because knowing and using the correct words is such an important aspect of being a good writer, vocabulary has always been a vital part of my studies.

Growing up, I mostly learned vocabulary from reading, noticing new words, and then trying them out in my own speech and writing. I hope to mimic that style of learning here. Students will quit memorizing and dictating vocabulary when we stop making them learn with that outdated and inefficient strategy. They need to have a vested interest in expanding their knowledge base with words they will use in their everyday language.

This book offers them that opportunity and helps them gain true word mastery.

HOW TO USE THIS BOOK

It's important to understand the type of vocabulary students should be learning. There are three tiers of vocabulary that support students:

- **Tier One** comprises basic vocabulary that we read and use every day. These are fundamental words that students learn in early grades.
- **Tier Two** is made up of high-frequency words that are typically used in chapter books and our everyday speech. These words vary from grade level to grade level.
- **Tier Three** words are used infrequently and are typically domain-specific words, often used in professions.

This vocabulary workbook is made up of Tier Two words that sixth graders are expected to know, understand, and use—words that sixth-grade students will frequently come across in their reading and writing. By gaining a stronger understanding of these words, your students will become stronger readers and writers with well-rounded vocabularies.

The format of this book encourages students to think about the words and not just memorize them, which is a much better structure than the old practice of copying words from a dictionary. With all 180 words at their fingertips, students can take control of their education and jump from one section to the next as needed.

FOR PARENTS AND TEACHERS

This vocabulary resource is a great way to enhance your student's language, as well as your own. It includes 36 weeks of lessons that will work great during the school year or summer break.

It's ideal for the learner to complete the lessons and accompanying activities with an adult who encourages them to use these words in their everyday vocabulary. But please allow the student to determine the pace of these lessons. They should be comfortable integrating new vocabulary into their vernacular. If they struggle to use these new words, begin parroting definitions, or forget words from previous lessons, please slow down and focus on learning the words and using them while you're speaking. Some of these activities even involve them asking *you* questions!

This is a great opportunity to have some fun and spark authentic connections about new vocabulary. Please embrace it and make learning fun! Words have power, and by expanding your learners' vocabularies, you are empowering them as individuals. Thank you for supporting this resource.

THE LESSONS

LESSON 1

Try to determine each word's meaning by how it is used in each sentence.

1. I didn't love the book I was reading, so I decided to **abandon** it and start a new one.

2. I can tell which of my friends are the most **genuine** because they take the time to ask me how I'm doing, no matter what.

3. Instead of relying on rainwater, farms try to **irrigate** their land to nourish the crops.

4. We had to **navigate** our way out of the woods without a compass so it took us longer than we thought it would.

5. We were excited to **reinforce** our blanket fort with extra string and tape to make it stronger.

How would you define the following?

abandon: _____

_____

genuine: _____

_____

irrigate: _____

_____

navigate: _____

_____

reinforce: _____

_____

Check your answers against the correct definitions in the back of the book. Then return to complete the next two activities.

KEEP IT CLOZE

Fill in the following blanks based on your new knowledge of the word definitions.

1. After hitting my leg by accident, Zyquan gave me a very kind and _____ apology so I forgave him immediately and understood that he didn't mean to do it.

2. I don't love **navigating** through my city, but I'm willing to do it if it means I can go see _____.

3. There are many ways to water crops, but it's easiest to _____ them.

4. There are certain foods that I will always **abandon** on my plate because I just don't care for them, like _____.

5. I was nervous walking on the dock because a wooden board was loose, but my dad used a hammer and some nails to _____ it and make it stronger.

CONTINUED >>

ASK AND ANSWERED

To strengthen your verbal familiarity with each word, ask a parent, sibling, or friend each of these questions.

1. To learn a new word, what do you do to **reinforce** it in your vocabulary?

2. Have you ever had to **abandon** a grocery cart at the grocery store?

3. Do you think farms can survive without **irrigation**?

4. Do you think a pet's love is the most **genuine**?

5. Do you need a map to **navigate** around your own city?

LESSON 2

Try to determine each word's meaning by how it is used in each sentence.

1. You can use your **discretion**, based on what sounds good to you, to decide what you want for dinner.

2. The rocky ledge was extremely **dangerous** to ride along, so Selah and Jonsie got off their bikes and slowly walked alongside of them to be safe.

3. The invention of e-mail and cell phones has allowed family and friends to stay in better **communication** with each other by making it very easy to talk to each other.

4. When you line up historical events on a timeline, you want to make sure they're in **chronological** order, so nobody is confused about the sequence of events.

5. The **government** is a system that helps citizens stay organized and follow the law.

How would you define the following?

discretion: _____

_____

dangerous: _____

_____

communication: _____

_____

CONTINUED >>

chronological: _____

_____

government: _____

_____

Check your answers against the correct definitions in the back of the book. Then return to complete the next two activities.

DIGGING FOR ROOTS

Complete the exercise based on the original roots you've learned for each word.

Word parts often change the meaning of the word. Check out the following examples and then think of your own word with that same word part.

The vocabulary words **discretion** and **communication** both end in -*tion*, a Middle English stem meaning "the result of." For example, **communication** is the result of **communicating**. Think of two other words you know that end in -*tion* and write them below. Then write the definition of your two new words.

starvation → *the result of starving*

_____ → _____

_____ → _____

Dangerous ends in -*ous*, a suffix that means "full of." For example, **dangerous** means "full of danger." What other words you know that end in -*ous*? Write them below. Then write how -*ous* changes the word.

poisonous → *full of poison*

_____ → _____

_____ → _____

SAME THING, DIFFERENT WORD

Using the vocabulary words from this lesson, find the synonym for each of the following words.

1. threatening → _____

2. sequential → _____

3. authority → _____

4. responsibility → _____

5. conversation → _____

LESSON 3

Try to determine each word's meaning by how it is used in each sentence.

1. My neighbor was kind enough to **accommodate** me by including me on their drive to school, so I could get a ride on the days my grandma couldn't drive me.

2. I could tell that Matthew's story was **exaggerated** when he started talking about the extremely large elephants he saw on his recent trip to the zoo. I know that all the elephants at our zoo are only babies!

3. I plan to take my money and **invest** it in a new pizza shop to help them open. This will make even more money when they succeed.

4. I think the best **strategy** for catching hermit crabs at the beach is to wait until the tide goes out and there are small pools of water all over the sand. Then it is easy to find the hermit crabs!

5. I wasn't sure what restaurant would be chosen when we started the meeting, but the **verdict** was easy; almost everyone wanted sushi instead of pizza!

How would you define the following?

accommodate: _____

_____

exaggerated: _____

_____

invest: _____

_____

strategy: _____

_____

verdict: _____

_____

Check your answers against the correct definitions in the back of the book.
Then return to complete the next two activities.

OPPOSING VIEWS

Using the vocabulary words from this lesson, find the antonym for
each of the following words.

1. deadlock → _____

2. minimize → _____

3. disinvest → _____

4. inconvenience → _____

5. oversight → _____

CONTINUED ››

CATEGORICALLY THINKING

Find the vocabulary word that best belongs with each group of words.

Example:

Vocabulary Word → **arrogant**

1. vain   *2. smug*   *3. aloof*

Vocabulary Word → _____
1. plan   2. design   3. scheme

Vocabulary Word → _____
1. answer   2. conclusion   3. decision

Vocabulary Word → _____
1. lend   2. spend   3. devote

Vocabulary Word → _____
1. fabricate   2. amplify   3. emphasize

Vocabulary Word → _____
1. welcome   2. entertain   3. shelter

LESSON 4

Try to determine each word's meaning by how it is used in each sentence.

1. It was easy to **calculate** my total at the store once I knew that each shirt cost only two dollars.

2. My mom is always trying to **embarrass** me when she drops me off at soccer practice. She plays children's songs as loud as she can, making me blush.

3. The firemen were so **heroic** for rushing into the burning building to save the puppies.

4. I had to find the **origin** of the nasty rumor about me so I could stop it from spreading any further.

5. I loved this book so much that as soon as I finished it, I passed it off to my cousin Laurie and quickly **paraphrased** it so she would know what it was about.

How would you define the following?

calculate: _____

_____

embarrass: _____

_____

heroic: _____

_____

CONTINUED >>

origin: _____

_____

paraphrased: _____

_____

Check your answers against the correct definitions in the back of the book. Then return to complete the next two activities.

KEEP IT CLOZE

Fill in the following blanks based on your new knowledge of the word definitions.

1.   The **origin** of many words is from _____.

2.   I was sure that the cashier had _____ my total incorrectly but I was too nervous to say anything, so I overpaid for my purchase.

3.   I am not easily **embarrassed** but I will always try to hide my face when _____.

4.   I have friends who are so **heroic**! They are always _____.

5.   During a test, my least favorite part is when we have to read something and then retell it by _____ it.

4

CATEGORICALLY THINKING

Find the vocabulary word that best belongs with each group of words.

Vocabulary Word → _____
1. connection   2. root   3. ancestry

Vocabulary Word → _____
1. annoy   2. disturb   3. fluster

Vocabulary Word → _____
1. count   2. measure   3. tally

Vocabulary Word → _____
1. rehash   2. rendering   3. summary

Vocabulary Word → _____
1. noble   2. courageous   3. gutsy

LESSON 5

Try to determine each word's meaning by how it is used in each sentence.

1. It is a huge **benefit** to have a parent who understands calculus when you bring home your confusing homework.

2. I will miss the **familiar** feeling of our old home that I grew up in. Now that we're moving to a new state and house, I will have to explore a new place.

3. My friend Brian has a great sense of **humor**. Every time he says something, I tend to burst out laughing because it's so funny!

4. My favorite season is spring because the tadpoles come out then! My friend Brianne **knows** everything about tadpoles, and I love to ask her all my questions and learn about everything I can about them.

5. I saw a picture of a dog online that is so cute, but I cannot find the **source** of the image to learn more about that dog.

How would you define the following?

benefit: _____

_____

familiar: _____

_____

humor: _____

_____

knows: _____

_____

source: _____

_____

Check your answers against the correct definitions in the back of the book. Then return to complete the next two activities.

ASK AND ANSWERED

To strengthen your verbal familiarity with each word, ask a parent, sibling, or friend each of these questions.

1. Who has the best sense of **humor** in our family?

2. Do you think we would **benefit** from adding another child to our family?

3. What is the **source** of our family's income?

4. Do you **know** a lot about outer space?

5. Are you **familiar** with the most popular television show right now?

CONTINUED >>

SAME THING, DIFFERENT WORD

Using the vocabulary words from this lesson, find the synonym for each of the following words.

1. awareness → _____

2. beginning → _____

3. wit → _____

4. accustomed → _____

5. gain → _____

LESSON 6

Try to determine each word's meaning by how it is used in each sentence.

1. I was so **dissatisfied** with my food, I had to order something else and throw my original plate in the garbage.

2. Using my tape measure, I carefully measured each **dimension** of the room so I would know which wall would fit my bed and which would fit my dresser.

3. For my birthday, I'm allowed to spend a **maximum** of $75 on anything I want as long as I don't go over my limit.

4. I gave my brother a **tentative** smile as our grandpa took his first steps without a cane. I didn't want to get our hopes up too high for just a few steps.

5. Have you ever gone to watch people run a marathon? I love how there are so many people who show up to **encourage** the runners, especially at the end when the runners are getting tired and need more support.

How would you define the following?

dissatisfied: _____

_____

dimension: _____

_____

maximum: _____

_____

CONTINUED >>

tentative: _____

_____

encourage: _____

_____

Check your answers against the correct definitions in the back of the book. Then return to complete the next two activities.

DIGGING FOR ROOTS

Complete the exercise based on the original roots you've learned for each word.

Word parts often change the meaning of the word. Check out the following examples and then think of your own word with that same word part.

Dissatisfied begins with the prefix *dis-*, which means "negative" or "opposite." For example, **dissatisfied** is the opposite of **satisfied**. Think of two other words you know that begin with *dis-* and write them below. Then write the definition of your two new words.

disappear → the opposite of appear

_____ → _____

_____ → _____

The suffix *-ion* is often used to turn a verb into a noun. For example, the verb **decide** becomes **decision** when you add *-ion*. Change the following verbs into nouns by adding *-ion*.

1. vacate → _____

2. discuss → _____

3. meditate → _____

4. explode → _____

OPPOSING VIEWS

Using the vocabulary words from this lesson, find the antonym for each of the following words.

1. segment → _____

2. annoy → _____

3. decisive → _____

4. pleased → _____

5. smallest → _____

LESSON 7

Try to determine each word's meaning by how it is used in each sentence.

1. Our school is ruled by a **democracy**, so every year we vote for the class president we think will do the best job.

2. Jen always checks out the weather **forecast** in the morning so she knows what to expect the rest of the day and what clothes she should wear.

3. My dog is always on **guard**, making sure I'm not in any danger from the local mail carrier or other dogs walking by.

4. Piranhas are **hostile** fish that like to attack and bite other fish and humans. They scare many people!

5. I love to visit a local **museum** when I'm in a new city because it allows me to learn about historical artifacts.

How would you define the following?

democracy: _____

_____

forecast: _____

_____

guard: _____

_____

hostile: _____

_____

museum: _____

_____

Check your answers against the correct definitions in the back of the book. Then return to complete the next two activities.

KEEP IT CLOZE

Fill in the following blanks based on your new knowledge of the word definitions.

1. After he called me a rude name, my feelings toward Lachlan were rather _____ and not very kind.

2. I think it's important to put certain items, like _____, in a safe so they are **guarded** from enemies.

3. _____ is a country ruled by **democracy**.

4. My favorite _____ to visit are the ones with famous artworks, like the *Mona Lisa*.

5. I _____ that this weekend's weather will be perfect.

CONTINUED >>

ASK AND ANSWERED

To strengthen your verbal familiarity with each word, ask a parent, sibling, or friend each of these questions.

1. What **museum** have you always wanted to visit?

2. Do you think it's important for a country to be ruled by a **democracy**?

3. What animals do you think are most **hostile**?

4. What do you **forecast** we will do this weekend?

5. Do you have anything that you think is important enough to **guard**?

LESSON 8

Try to determine each word's meaning by how it is used in each sentence.

1. Although Parker knew how to do multiplication, he struggled solving the **equation** and couldn't get the numbers to make sense.

2. I didn't realize how **extensive** the hurricane damage was until we drove into town and saw that every single house needed repairs.

3. I knew James was **guilty** of stealing a piece of gum because I saw him take it, but I was scared to tell our teacher because I knew James would get in trouble.

4. My little brother, Luke, grew so **gradually** over the year that I never even saw a change but was amazed at how big he got!

5. Bill Gates is **generous** with his money, giving millions of dollars to charities and those who need help.

How would you define the following?

equation: _____

_____

extensive: _____

_____

guilty: _____

_____

CONTINUED >>

gradually: _____

_____

generous: _____

_____

Check your answers against the correct definitions in the back of the book. Then return to complete the next two activities.

DIGGING FOR ROOTS

Complete the exercise based on the original roots you've learned for each word.

Word parts often change the meaning of the word. Check out the following examples and then think of your own word with that same word part.

Suffix: *-ty*: a suffix that denotes a specific quality

guilty → *denotes guilt*
respectability → *denotes being respectable*

_____ → _____

Prefix: *grad-*: a prefix meaning "step"

gradual → *going slowly, step by step*
gradient → *a degree of incline surface*

_____ → _____

SAME THING, DIFFERENT WORD

Using the vocabulary words from this lesson, find the synonym for each of the following words.

1. progressive → _____

2. voluminous → _____

3. liable → _____

4. comparison → _____

5. unselfish → _____

LESSON 9

Try to determine each word's meaning by how it is used in each sentence.

1. My favorite nonprofit organization is one that works to **abolish** hunger and homelessness in our town.

2. I have to **analyze** our budget before I know if we can afford another vacation.

3. O'Ryan was tired of the rude **behavior** in the city so he moved back to his hometown, where everyone was friendly and welcoming.

4. I am a good **citizen**, so I follow the rules in my town and always vote for our town officials!

5. I had to **persuade** my parents to lend me money for a movie ticket Friday night by promising them I would work on Saturday to repay them.

How would you define the following?

abolish: _____

_____

analyze: _____

_____

behavior: _____

_____

citizen: _____

_____

persuade: _____

_____

Check your answers against the correct definitions in the back of the book. Then return to complete the next two activities.

OPPOSING VIEWS

Using the vocabulary words from this lesson, find the antonym for each of the following words.

1. foreigner → _____

2. approve → _____

3. discourage → _____

4. misconduct → _____

5. neglect → _____

CONTINUED >>

CATEGORICALLY THINKING

Find the vocabulary word that best belongs with each group of words.

Vocabulary Word → _____

1. act   2. conduct   3. demeanor

Vocabulary Word → _____

1. evaluate   2. consider   3. investigate

Vocabulary Word → _____

1. coax   2. influence   3. sway

Vocabulary Word → _____

1. eradicate   2. terminate   3. dissolve

Vocabulary Word → _____

1. inhabitant   2. resident   3. villager

LESSON 10

Try to determine each word's meaning by how it is used in each sentence.

1. Once I **accomplish** my goal of writing four pages each day, I will finally be able to get my book printed!

2. I read **approximately** 45 books this past year. I kept track of most of them!

3. I was completely **exhausted** after running around chasing my toddler nephew all day. He didn't stop!

4. My best friends all have a similar **quality**; they're very kind and outgoing.

5. The birds **swarm** the skies every fall as they travel south to warmer weather.

How would you define the following?

accomplish: _____

_____

approximately: _____

_____

exhausted: _____

_____

quality: _____

_____

CONTINUED >>

swarm: _____

_____

Check your answers against the correct definitions in the back of the book. Then return to complete the next two activities.

Fill in the following blanks based on your new knowledge of the word definitions.

1. I wanted my bicycle fixed but wasn't sure if I could afford it. They gave me an _____ price and if it stays around there, I know it would be okay.

2. I saw a **swarm** of _____ along the river during sunrise.

3. My best friend has the greatest **qualities**, but my favorite is her _____.

4. I have so many goals I want to **accomplish**, like _____.

5. Going for a run with my neighbor's dog is _____. I always need a nap afterward!

CATEGORICALLY THINKING

Find the vocabulary word that best belongs with each group of words.

Vocabulary Word → _____
1. flock   2. crowd   3. horde

Vocabulary Word → _____
1. fatigue   2. overwork   3. weaken

Vocabulary Word → _____
1. estimate   2. near   3. resemble

Vocabulary Word → _____
1. achieve   2. conclude   3. attain

Vocabulary Word → _____
1. aspect   2. character   3. trait

LESSON 11

Try to determine each word's meaning by how it is used in each sentence.

1.   My dog will **accumulate** treats and bury them under his favorite tree in our backyard instead of enjoying them when we give them to him.

2.   The air in Arizona is extremely **arid**; it always makes my skin really tight and dry.

3.   My friend, Maegan, never **ceases** to amaze me with the funny things that come out of her mouth!

4.   It takes a lot of **courage** to tell your parents the truth, especially when you know they'll be upset, but it's so worth it.

5.   I could **remain** at the beach for hours and hours if my family let me. It's so soothing and I love listening to the waves.

How would you define the following?

accumulate: _____

_____

arid: _____

_____

ceases: _____

_____

courage: _____

_____

remain: _____

_____

Check your answers against the correct definitions in the back of the book. Then return to complete the next two activities.

To strengthen your verbal familiarity with each word, ask a parent, sibling, or friend each of these questions.

1. What is your favorite candy to **accumulate** during the holidays?

2. Is the air in your home **arid**?

3. What is a habit you wish to **cease**?

4. What does **courage** mean to you?

5. How many days **remain** until your birthday?

OPPOSING VIEWS

Using the vocabulary words from this lesson, find the antonym for each of the following words.

1. begin → _____

2. humid → _____

3. cowardice → _____

4. decrease → _____

5. leave → _____

LESSON 12

Try to determine each word's meaning by how it is used in each sentence.

1. Before my dog, Bailey, could stay at the dog camp overnight, we had to prove that he was **obedient** and would listen to the camp counselors.

2. Laurie, Miguel, and Allen made a **unanimous** decision to explore the caves on their hike instead of leaving early. They all agreed that the caves would be more fun.

3. I love to **compose** poems in my spare time. They're quick and fun to write!

4. Nobody **opposed** Bruno in the election, so it was easy for him to win!

5. Sarah got everyone's attention and **declared** that it was time to eat supper and they should all go into the other room.

How would you define the following?

obedient: _____

_____

unanimous: _____

_____

compose: _____

_____

opposed: _____

_____

_____

Check your answers against the correct definitions in the back of the book. Then return to complete the next two activities.

DIGGING FOR ROOTS

Complete the exercises based on the original roots you've learned for each word.

Word parts often change the meaning of the word. Check out the following examples and then think of your own word with that same word part.

The root word *anim* in **unanimous** means "life, mind, or spirit." What other words do you know that have *anim*? Write two below. Then write the definition of your two new words, keeping in mind the meaning of the root word.

unanimous → thinking of one mind
anime → a Japanese style of animation with a lot of action
animalistic → showing the characteristic of an animal

_____ → _____

_____ → _____

CONTINUED >>

THE LESSONS   35

The prefixes *co-*, *com-*, and *con-* all mean "with" or "together." For example, **compose** means "to put together." What other words do you know that have *co-*, *com-*, or *con-*? Write four of them below. Then write what that word means, keeping in mind the meaning of the prefix.

combine → *to put two things together*
committee → *a group of people who come together*
  and meet to discuss a topic

_____ → _____

_____ → _____

_____ → _____

_____ → _____

OPPOSING VIEWS

Using the vocabulary words from this lesson, find the antonym for each of the following words.

1. suppress → _____

2. demolish → _____

3. disloyal → _____

4. divided → _____

5. agree → _____

LESSON 13

Try to determine each word's meaning by how it is used in each sentence.

1. The Great Pyramids in Egypt are considered **ancient**.

2. Lisa and Wilder were excited to see the Celtic **artifacts** from the museum. There were many tools and devices that villagers created and used thousands of years ago.

3. The lake by our house is so **gigantic** that it takes three hours to walk all the way around it.

4. I have a friend who can **manipulate** any situation, making everyone want to do exactly what she wants to do.

5. Quinn was a **curious** child, always wanting to crawl toward new noises and see what was happening.

How would you define the following?

ancient: _____

_____

artifacts: _____

_____

gigantic: _____

_____

manipulate: _____

_____

CONTINUED >>

curious: _____

_____

Check your answers against the correct definitions in the back of the book. Then return to complete the next two activities.

KEEP IT CLOZE

Fill in the following blanks based on your new knowledge of the word definitions.

1. I love to see the fascinating _____ at our town's museum.

2. The most **gigantic** pumpkin I've ever seen was _____ pounds.

3. I am extremely **curious** to learn more about _____.

4. My dog can easily _____ us by whining at our feet when we have food, making us believe he needs more food, even if he doesn't.

5. The _____ dinosaur fossil was amazing to see in person. I could just envision how different life was when dinosaurs roamed our Earth.

ASK AND ANSWERED

To strengthen your verbal familiarity with each word, ask a parent, sibling, or friend each of these questions.

1. Have you ever felt **manipulated** by someone?

2. Are you more **curious** to learn about outer space or the rainforests? Why?

3. Are there any items from your childhood that feel **ancient** now? What are they and can you share a picture of them?

4. What **artifact** from our past would you like to see in person?

5. What is the most **gigantic** amusement park you've ever seen? Would you want to visit there?

LESSON 14

Try to determine each word's meaning by how it is used in each sentence.

1. Gabriella's dad is **consistently** late to pick her up from school, so she doesn't even bother to leave the building until 15 minutes after everyone else.

2. The side of the mountain was completely **vertical**, making it extremely challenging to climb up without a rope and footholds.

3. Ross' hands were **massive**, which made it easy to pick tomatoes and complete work around their family farm.

4. After doing a blind taste test, Matthew and MacKenzie agreed that the barbecue-flavored chips were far **superior** to the vinegar chips; they ate all of the barbecue chips in no time!

5. After waiting for what felt like forever, Jim grew **impatient** and left Jody in the arcade before she was finished playing games.

How would you define the following?

consistently: _____

_____

vertical: _____

_____

massive: _____

_____

superior: _____

_____

impatient: _____

_____

Check your answers against the correct definitions in the back of the book. Then return to complete the next two activities.

DIGGING FOR ROOTS

Complete the exercise based on the original roots you've learned for each word.

Word parts often change the meaning of the word. Check out the following examples and then think of your own word with that same word part.

The suffix -*ent* describes a process. For example, **consistent** means "the process of consisting." What other words do you know that end in -*ent*? Write two below. Then write the definition of your new words.

dependent → *the process of depending on someone*

_____ → _____

_____ → _____

CONTINUED >>

SAME THING, DIFFERENT WORD

Using the vocabulary words from this lesson, find the synonym for each of the following words.

1. anxious → _____

2. better → _____

3. steep → _____

4. dependable → _____

5. immense → _____

LESSON 15

Try to determine each word's meaning by how it is used in each sentence.

1. Dennison quickly learned that there was a **consequence** for not listening to his parents; he had to clean out the shed, garage, and attic all by himself.

2. When Tricia fell out of the raft and started getting pulled down the stream, Cameron had to resort to **drastic** measures to save her. He quickly jumped out of the raft with an extra life jacket and wrapped it around her waist.

3. I forgot to **mention** to our server that I wanted my food to go, so we had to wait an extra five minutes for them to wrap it up.

4. Matthew has great **rhythm**; he can hear a song and remember the beat later.

5. The volunteers at the parade are a big **service** to the community. They help organize and plan everything, making sure the parade runs smoothly.

How would you define the following?

consequence: _____

_____

drastic: _____

_____

mention: _____

_____

CONTINUED >>

rhythm: _____

_____

service: _____

_____

Check your answers against the correct definitions in the back of the book. Then return to complete the next two activities.

OPPOSING VIEWS

Using the vocabulary words from this lesson, find the antonym for each of the following words.

1. omission → _____

2. discord → _____

3. insignificant → _____

4. forceless → _____

5. cause → _____

CATEGORICALLY THINKING

Find the vocabulary word that best belongs with each group
of words.

Vocabulary Word → _____
1. flow   2. pattern   3. tempo

Vocabulary Word → _____
1. employment   2. maintenance   3. assistance

Vocabulary Word → _____
1. aftermath   2. effect   3. repercussion

Vocabulary Word → _____
1. dire   2. forceful   3. harsh

Vocabulary Word → _____
1. comment   2. utterance   3. notification

LESSON 16

Try to determine each word's meaning by how it is used in each sentence.

1. Our Sunday night dinner at Brianne's house is so fun. Everyone is supposed to **contribute** one dish so there's enough dinner for all of us to enjoy!

2. The kitten was already kind; **moreover**, she loved to snuggle and play with us.

3. I love to listen to books when they've been **narrated** by the author; the story sounds so good read by them!

4. Whenever I get a glass of water, I always ask for a lemon so I can **squeeze** the juice into my glass because I like the lemon flavor in my water.

5. Colleen enjoyed going on a **quest** to find her new favorite book at the bookstore.

How would you define the following?

contribute: _____

_____

moreover: _____

_____

narrated: _____

_____

squeeze: _____

_____

quest: _____

_____

Check your answers against the correct definitions in the back of the book. Then return to complete the next two activities.

KEEP IT CLOZE

Fill in the following blanks based on your new knowledge of the word definitions.

1. If I could have anyone **narrate** my favorite book, it would be

_____.

2. My grandmother gives the best hugs because she

_____ us so tight and makes us feel

very loved.

3. I do love to read; _____, I really love to write.

4. Chris and Lauren loved to _____ their travel

stories to the local magazine.

5. Matilda took off one day and went on a _____

around her neighborhood to find new friends.

CONTINUED >>

CATEGORICALLY THINKING

Find the vocabulary word that best belongs with each group of words.

Vocabulary Word → _____

1. add   2. share   3. supply

Vocabulary Word → _____

1. compress   2. pinch   3. wring

Vocabulary Word → _____

1. adventure   2. expedition   3. journey

Vocabulary Word → _____

1. recount   2. chronicle   3. recite

Vocabulary Word → _____

1. in addition to   2. also   3. furthermore

LESSON 17

Try to determine each word's meaning by how it is used in each sentence.

1. Martina was quick to **adapt** her dinner plans of grilled chicken when she learned her guests were vegetarian and wouldn't eat meat.

2. The old man at the end of the street had a **peculiar** habit of collecting birdhouses.

3. I love to share my favorite inspirational **quotes** with my friends when they are feeling sad.

4. When Haley goes out to run, she has to start slow or else she has a ton of **tension** in her legs, making it challenging to move.

5. The **variable** weather makes it difficult to choose an outfit each day. I never know if it will be cold or warm.

How would you define the following?

adapt: _____

_____

peculiar: _____

_____

quotes: _____

_____

CONTINUED ›››

tension: _____

_____

variable: _____

_____

Check your answers against the correct definitions in the back of the book. Then return to complete the next two activities.

ASK AND ANSWERED

To strengthen your verbal familiarity with each word, ask a parent, sibling, or friend each of these questions.

1.   What is the most **peculiar** thing you've ever eaten?

2.   What are your favorite **variables** to experiment with in baking?

3.   Why is there a lot of **tension** between two teams that play each other?

4.   What is your favorite **quote** from a famous person?

5.   How would you **adapt** to a quick change in weather if you were out on a hike?

SAME THING, DIFFERENT WORD

Using the vocabulary words from this lesson, find the synonym for each of the following words.

1. fluctuating → _____

2. citation → _____

3. accommodate → _____

4. unique → _____

5. strain → _____

LESSON 18

Try to determine each word's meaning by how it is used in each sentence.

1.   We had to **vacate** the dance floor when the DJ left because the music was done for the night.

2.   When Eddie wakes up in the morning, he has extremely **unruly** hair that refuses to stay down with hair gel or water.

3.   Kevin **transferred** all of his money to a savings account so he could start saving for college.

4.   It's hard to **transport** gifts for family members when you only have a little space in your suitcase.

5.   The **monotonous** sound of the train wheels click-clacking down the track quickly put Braella to sleep.

How would you define the following?

vacate: _____

_____

unruly: _____

_____

transferred: _____

_____

transport: _____

_____

monotonous: _____

_____

Check your answers against the correct definitions in the back of the book. Then return to complete the next two activities.

DIGGING FOR ROOTS

Complete the exercise based on the original roots you've learned for each word.

Word parts often change the meaning of the word. Check out the following examples and then think of your own word with that same word part.

The word part *vac* means "empty." For example, the word **vacate** means "to give up possession." Think of three other words that have *vac* in them and write them and their meaning below.

evacuate → *the result of vacating*

_____ → _____

_____ → _____

_____ → _____

CONTINUED >>

The word part *trans* means "across, through, or changing." For example, the word **transfer** means "to move from one place to another." Think of three other words that have *trans* in them and write them and their meaning below.

transport → *to carry from one place to another*

_____ → _____

_____ → _____

_____ → _____

OPPOSING VIEWS

Using the vocabulary words from this lesson, find the antonym for each of the following words.

1. occupy → _____

2. eventful → _____

3. agreeable → _____

4. drop → _____

5. stationed → _____

LESSON 19

Try to determine each word's meaning by how it is used in each sentence.

1.   It was hard to stay hydrated because we did not have an **adequate** amount of water to drink on our hike.

2.   Our school dress code is so strict that it's hard to find a short sleeve shirt that's **appropriate** to wear to school.

3.   I love listening to my parents' friends **recount** stories from when they were growing up.

4.   I love sour candy, but green sour candies **specifically** are my favorite.

5.   My friend Dan has the best **trait**; he is very kind and always asks me how I'm doing!

How would you define the following?

adequate: _____

_____

appropriate: _____

_____

recount: _____

_____

specifically: _____

_____

CONTINUED >>

trait: _____

_____

Check your answers against the correct definitions in the back of the book. Then return to complete the next two activities.

KEEP IT CLOZE

Fill in the following blanks based on your new knowledge of the word definitions.

1. I need my _____ pen for writing or else it's hard for me to get motivated.

2. It is not **appropriate** to wear a _____ to a wedding.

3. I think the most important **trait** to have is _____.

4. Joe always has an _____ number of snacks at his house for everyone to enjoy.

5. It's hard to **recount** a story when you're _____.

ASK AND ANSWERED

To strengthen your verbal familiarity with each word, ask a parent, sibling, or friend each of these questions.

1. What's your favorite childhood memory to **recount**?

2. Do you think I have an **adequate** amount of homework?

3. Is there a **specific** food you dislike?

4. Do you think cats or dogs have better **traits**?

5. What do you think is an **appropriate** amount of money to spend on a fancy gourmet meal?

LESSON 20

Try to determine each word's meaning by how it is used in each sentence.

1. The **foundation** of our fort was built on uneven ground so it's not very solid or safe.

2. Craig did such an **outstanding** job on his science fair project that he was awarded first prize and was asked to help younger students learn about his research.

3. After the large snowfall, I wanted to go out for a walk, but it was too **treacherous**. There were too many trees down and the roads were icy.

4. Katlyn was so nervous about the **selection** process for her upcoming promotion, but she knew that she deserved the job and hoped they would add her to the list.

5. When baking a cake for her friend, Channing ran out of regular milk and had to **substitute** almond milk instead. Luckily the cake still turned out great.

How would you define the following?

foundation: _____

_____

outstanding: _____

_____

treacherous: _____

_____

selection: _____

_____

substitute: _____

_____

Check your answers against the correct definitions in the back of the book. Then return to complete the next two activities.

DIGGING FOR ROOTS

Complete the exercise based on the original roots you've learned for each word.

Word parts often change the meaning of the word. Check out the following examples and then think of your own words with that same word part.

-tion: changes the word to mean the result of a condition

> *foundation* → *where something is founded*
> *selection* → *when something is selected*
> *action* → *when something is acted upon*

_____ → _____

_____ → _____

CONTINUED >>

sub-: a prefix that means "under, below, or beneath"

substitute → *something that serves under the real item*

submerge → *to put something under water*

_____ → _____

_____ → _____

SAME THING, DIFFERENT WORD

Using the vocabulary words from this lesson, find the synonym for each of the following words.

1. exceptional → _____

2. base → _____

3. choice → _____

4. replacement → _____

5. slippery → _____

LESSON 21

Try to determine each word's meaning by how it is used in each sentence.

1. It was pure **anguish** having to give our cat away when we moved, but I knew her life on the farm would be much better than our new life in a small city apartment.

2. Wilder started his own produce **business** selling homegrown fruits at the entrance of his neighborhood when he was just seven years old.

3. Before they went outside to meet some friends, Kelsey quickly told Brian the **gist** of her day so he could understand why she was so upset.

4. Nate was shocked that Melissa would **insist** on adding another picture to their project poster. He thought it already had enough, but he drew another one anyway.

5. On Monday, Carter couldn't take it anymore and decided to **revolt** against another reading test. He read a book in the corner instead, which really upset his teacher.

How would you define the following?

anguish: _____

_____

business: _____

_____

gist: _____

_____

CONTINUED >>

insist: _____

_____

revolt: _____

_____

Check your answers against the correct definitions in the back of the book. Then return to complete the next two activities.

OPPOSING VIEWS

Using the vocabulary words from this lesson, find the antonym for each of the following words.

1. hobby → _____

2. ignore → _____

3. surrender → _____

4. delight → _____

5. extremely detailed → _____

CATEGORICALLY THINKING

Find the vocabulary word that best belongs with each group of words.

Vocabulary Word → _____
1. agony   2. grief   3. heartache

Vocabulary Word → _____
1. defy   2. overthrow   3. disagree

Vocabulary Word → _____
1. summary   2. briefing   3. significant

Vocabulary Word → _____
1. assert   2. stand firm   3. demand

Vocabulary Word → _____
1. corporation   2. institution   3. partnership

LESSON 22

Try to determine each word's meaning by how it is used in each sentence.

1. Every autumn I get a horrible **cough** from the changing weather, making it uncomfortable to breathe.

2. It's important that we **factor** in the different shades of blue when we try to find the perfect paint color for our kitchen.

3. Warren was the perfect **height** for hiding cookies in the pantry, just high enough that his friends couldn't reach them.

4. Many medicines are good for you, but if you take too much of a specific medicine, it can be **toxic** for your body and make you feel worse.

5. Kathy couldn't see the dolphins in the ocean from her **viewpoint**, but she was able to see the waves crashing down on the sand.

How would you define the following?

cough: _____

_____

factor: _____

_____

height: _____

_____

toxic: _____

_____

viewpoint: _____

_____

Check your answers against the correct definitions in the back of the book. Then return to complete the next two activities.

KEEP IT CLOZE

Fill in the following blanks based on your new knowledge of the word definitions.

1. I really like my **height**. I'm _____.

2. It's not the typical **viewpoint**, but I think _____ are better than dogs.

3. The worst _____ I've ever had was after I spent a week with my sick cousin.

4. I think it's important to _____ in the cost of flights as well as the timing of each flight when booking something.

5. I felt _____ when **toxic** chemicals were dumped into the river.

CONTINUED >>

22

CATEGORICALLY THINKING

Find the vocabulary word that best belongs with each group of words.

Vocabulary Word → _____
1. angle   2. direction   3. perspective

Vocabulary Word → _____
1. element   2. component   3. influence

Vocabulary Word → _____
1. deadly   2. harmful   3. lethal

Vocabulary Word → _____
1. elevation   2. peak   3. crest

Vocabulary Word → _____
1. ahem   2. hack   3. bark

LESSON 23

Try to determine each word's meaning by how it is used in each sentence.

1. In order to **conserve** water, we should turn off the faucet while we're brushing our teeth.

2. Matilda has a **knack** for waking up right before breakfast is ready.

3. Megan's goal of writing a book of her own in the new year was **lofty**, but she knew that if she worked hard enough, she would be able to finish it.

4. When Joe wants to stop at his favorite restaurant for a slice of their supreme pizza, he has to **negotiate** with his parents, offering to do extra chores in exchange for stopping.

5. My **philosophy** in life is to work hard now so I can be successful in my future career.

How would you define the following?

conserve: _____

_____

knack: _____

_____

lofty: _____

_____

CONTINUED >>

negotiate: _____

_____

philosophy: _____

_____

Check your answers against the correct definitions in the back of the book. Then return to complete the next two activities.

ASK AND ANSWERED

To strengthen your verbal familiarity with each word, ask a parent, sibling, or friend each of these questions.

1. Do you have a **knack** for playing a musical instrument? If so, which one? If not, which one do you wish you did?

2. Who is your favorite **philosopher**?

3. How can you **conserve** energy in your home better?

4. What is the best way to **negotiate** for more dessert after dinner?

5. Have you ever completed a task that seemed extremely **lofty** in the beginning? Tell me about it.

SAME THING, DIFFERENT WORD

Using the vocabulary words from this lesson, find the synonym for each of the following words.

1. towering → _____

2. preserve → _____

3. skill → _____

4. outlook → _____

5. haggle → _____

LESSON 24

Try to determine each word's meaning by how it is used in each sentence.

1. Judging by Dustin's **expression**, he was not expecting to see his mom at lunch today!

2. Lisa's dog, Bayliss, was so **ferocious** that they had to keep him on a leash at all times so he wouldn't get near another dog.

3. Patricia worked so hard to **influence** Cameron to walk to the park and play on the playground, but no matter what she said, Cameron didn't want to go.

4. Many people say that adding cinnamon to your food is an **effective** way to stay healthy and keep germs away.

5. Zachary was so confused about the **objective** of their baking lesson in math. Why were they baking cookies while learning about fractions?

How would you define the following?

expression: _____

_____

ferocious: _____

_____

influence: _____

_____

effective: _____

_____

objective: _____

_____

Check your answers against the correct definitions in the back of the book. Then return to complete the next two activities.

DIGGING FOR ROOTS

Complete the exercise based on the original roots you've learned for each word.

Word parts often change the meaning of the word. Check out the following examples and then think of your own word, or words, with that same word part.

-sion: changes the word to mean the result of an action

> *expression* → *the result of expressing*
> *comprehension* → *the result of comprehending*

_____ → _____

_____ → _____

CONTINUED >>

-ive: a suffix added to a word to create an adjective; from the Latin word *ivus* meaning "pertaining to"

effective → *to effect*

objective → *to object*

_____ → _____

_____ → _____

OPPOSING VIEWS

Using the vocabulary words from this lesson, find the antonym for each of the following words.

1. calm → _____

2. inefficient → _____

3. unfair → _____

4. suppression → _____

5. powerless → _____

LESSON 25

Try to determine each word's meaning by how it is used in each sentence.

1. The book's cover was extremely **alarming**. It was obviously a horror story and would be too scary for me to read.

2. I had the most **pleasant** morning with my friend Pamela, just walking around the mall and shopping for new clothes. It was exactly what I needed.

3. The new video games are extremely **realistic**. It's hard to tell what's fake and what's real sometimes!

4. I shared my **thesis** with the class before I started my science project. I wanted them to know what I was hoping to prove with my experiment.

5. My friends Jennifer and Brandon are so **vibrant**. They're always willing to go on an adventure and explore our city. After a day with them I always come home exhausted.

How would you define the following?

alarming: _____

_____

pleasant: _____

_____

realistic: _____

_____

CONTINUED >>

thesis: _____

_____

vibrant: _____

_____

Check your answers against the correct definitions in the back of the book. Then return to complete the next two activities.

KEEP IT CLOZE

Fill in the following blanks based on your new knowledge of the word definitions.

1. It's not very **realistic** to eat _____ every day.

2. I find it extremely _____ that Carter wanted to eat only broccoli and tomatoes for dinner tonight.

3. Blakely always wears the most **vibrant** colors, like _____.

4. Maegan presented her _____ to her friends, explaining to them how she hoped to find a way to cure hunger in the community.

5. For Nathan, the most _____ morning involved banana pancakes, hot chocolate, and lots of cartoons on TV.

ASK AND ANSWERED

To strengthen your verbal familiarity with each word, ask a parent, sibling, or friend each of these questions.

1. What do you think is the most **alarming** noise?

2. Who is your most **vibrant** person you know? What makes them so **vibrant**?

3. What's your idea of a **pleasant** place?

4. Do you enjoy writing **thesis** statements?

5. Do you think computer graphics in movies are **realistic** these days?

LESSON 26

Try to determine each word's meaning by how it is used in each sentence.

1. It's important to have a **balanced** meal, with a good amount of vegetables, protein, carbs, and even a little bit of dessert.

2. As I walked into the house, I heard a weird sound outside. I stepped **backward** to see what it could be and quickly saw it was just my neighbor starting his lawnmower.

3. My friend Matt can be so **awkward** around new people. He doesn't know what to say or how to act.

4. It's easy to **predict** the weather when you live on the ocean. You can see it coming really far out, so you know what will happen.

5. It's **ridiculous** that Heather and I don't have any classes together. We never get to see each other!

How would you define the following?

balanced: _____

_____

backward: _____

_____

awkward: _____

_____

predict: _____

_____

ridiculous: _____

_____

Check your answers against the correct definitions in the back of the book. Then return to complete the next two activities.

DIGGING FOR ROOTS

Complete the exercise based on the original roots you've learned for each word.

Word parts often change the meaning of the word. Check out the following examples and then think of your own words with that same word part.

-ward: denotes direction

> *backward* → *moving to the back*
> *toward* → *moving to something*

_____ → _____

_____ → _____

CONTINUED >>

pre-: means "before"

    predict → *to declare something before it happens*

    preview → *to see something before*

_____ → _____

_____ → _____

SAME THING, DIFFERENT WORD

Using the vocabulary words from this lesson, find the synonym for each of the following words.

1. reverse → _____

2. forecast → _____

3. absurd → _____

4. blundering → _____

5. stable → _____

LESSON 27

Try to determine each word's meaning by how it is used in each sentence.

1. We moved to the **adjacent** street so the stream wouldn't be able to reach our house every time it rained a lot.

2. Every time we go somewhere, Greg envisions a **catastrophe** happening and worries about everything we do until we're safe at home again.

3. Kate and Kelci make themselves **scarce** when it's time to do the chores. They know that if their mom can't find them, they won't have to do the work!

4. I found the perfect **solution** for getting to school. My dad drops me off on his way to work and I can read a book by my locker until class starts. It's much better than taking the bus every day.

5. Even though it was hot outside, Brooke could not stop **trembling** from the cold after swimming in the freezing lake.

How would you define the following?

adjacent: _____

_____

catastrophe: _____

_____

scarce: _____

_____

CONTINUED >>

solution: _____

_____

trembling: _____

_____

Check your answers against the correct definitions in the back of the book. Then return to complete the next two activities.

OPPOSING VIEWS

Using the vocabulary words from this lesson, find the antonym for each of the following words.

1. blessing → _____

2. stable → _____

3. detached → _____

4. problem → _____

5. plentiful → _____

CATEGORICALLY THINKING

Find the vocabulary word that best belongs with each group of words.

Vocabulary Word → _____

1. adjoining   2. bordering   3. neighboring

Vocabulary Word → _____

1. limited   2. sparse   3. sporadic

Vocabulary Word → _____

1. accident   2. calamity   3. fiasco

Vocabulary Word → _____

1. quiver   2. shudder   3. flutter

Vocabulary Word → _____

1. explanation   2. result   3. clarification

LESSON 28

Try to determine each word's meaning by how it is used in each sentence.

1. Max's **capacity** to love and care for his family seemed never-ending because he was always looking out for them and taking care of them.

2. After Cam showed up late, our soccer practice was **extended** and we had to run laps at the end.

3. While babysitting, Jayla had to continuously **retrieve** the ball that Arianna kept throwing out of her highchair.

4. After building an enormous tower out of blocks, Morgan and Wyatt had to **deconstruct** it and put all of the blocks away.

5. If they really want to succeed as gymnasts, Drew and Barrett need to **devote** at least 20 hours a week to practicing.

How would you define the following?

capacity: _____

_____

extended: _____

_____

retrieve: _____

_____

deconstruct: _____

_____

devote: _____

_____

Check your answers against the correct definitions in the back of the book. Then return to complete the next two activities.

KEEP IT CLOZE

Fill in the following blanks based on your new knowledge of the word definitions.

1. We tried to _____ the wooden dam in our backyard that is blocking the water from flowing through the stream.

2. Our principal may have a lot of power in school, but when we see him out at dinner, he has no _____ to punish us, even if he disagrees with our behavior.

3. In order to get better, I will **devote** more hours toward practicing _____.

4. Our dog loves to play fetch and _____ a ball over and over again.

5. When we have family in town for a holiday, we always have to _____ the table so everyone can fit around it.

CONTINUED >>

CATEGORICALLY THINKING

Find the vocabulary word that best belongs with each group of words.

Vocabulary Word → _____

1. recapture   2. recover   3. salvage

Vocabulary Word → _____

1. apply   2. dedicate   3. donate

Vocabulary Word → _____

1. enhance   2. expand   3. spread

Vocabulary Word → _____

1. quantity   2. scope   3. space

Vocabulary Word → _____

1. dismantle   2. dissect   3. unravel

LESSON 29

Try to determine each word's meaning by how it is used in each sentence.

1. I was so nervous when they started to **announce** the winners' names.
    I really wanted to hear them say my name!

2. Reagan absolutely loves to learn about **history**. She's fascinated
    by the different lifestyles and events that happened during her
    grandparents' lifetime.

3. Many families will **immigrate** to a different country if they do not feel safe
    living in their country.

4. Everyone laughed when Grant and Tanner showed up to the costume party
    wearing **similar** costumes, and then they took pictures together.

5. The **suspense** was overwhelming for Gabe as he waited to hear back
    about his test scores. He had studied so hard and needed to know his
    grade immediately.

How would you define the following?

announce: _____

_____

history: _____

_____

immigrate: _____

_____

CONTINUED >>

similar: _____

_____

suspense: _____

_____

Check your answers against the correct definitions in the back of the book. Then return to complete the next two activities.

ASK AND ANSWERED

To strengthen your verbal familiarity with each word, ask a parent, sibling, or friend each of these questions.

1. Would you ever want to **immigrate** to a country with a cold climate?

2. Do you enjoy movies with a lot of **suspense**?

3. What is the most important **announcement** you've ever made?

4. Have you ever witnessed **history** in the making? What happened?

5. Do you know anyone **similar** to you? If so, who? How are they **similar** to you?

SAME THING, DIFFERENT WORD

Using the vocabulary words from this lesson, find the synonym for each of the following words.

1. uncertainty → _____

2. identical → _____

3. move → _____

4. declare → _____

5. past → _____

LESSON 30

Try to determine each word's meaning by how it is used in each sentence.

1. We moved away from **civilization** and onto a farmland with multiple animals, acres of land, and zero neighbors.

2. The **conclusion** of the book was my favorite part. I was so happy to see the characters end up together.

3. Blake is so **confident** in himself. He always sets out to reach a goal and he accomplishes it quickly.

4. Corey uses her hands a lot when she speaks, which is nice because the movements are often **congruent** with the conversation.

5. At the beginning of the experiment, Brittany thought her **hypothesis** was correct. Unfortunately, as she learned more about the specimens, she realized it was incorrect.

How would you define the following?

civilization: _____

_____

conclusion: _____

_____

confident: _____

_____

congruent: _____

_____

hypothesis: _____

_____

Check your answers against the correct definitions in the back of the book.
Then return to complete the next two activities.

DIGGING FOR ROOTS

Complete the exercise based on the original roots you've learned for
each word.

Word parts often change the meaning of the word. Check out the
following examples and then think of your own words with that same
word part.

con-: means "with" or "together"

> *conclusion → to pull the end together*
> *congruent → with agreement*

_____ → _____

_____ → _____

_____ → _____

CONTINUED >>

OPPOSING VIEWS

Using the vocabulary words from this lesson, find the antonym for each of the following words.

1. disagreeable → _____

2. fact → _____

3. primitive → _____

4. beginning → _____

5. cowardly → _____

LESSON 31

Try to determine each word's meaning by how it is used in each sentence.

1. Gussie found it relaxing to sit and **construct** block towers with her two-year-old niece.

2. My friend Emily is an amazing **daughter** to her mother. She travels home to see and spends all holidays with her.

3. Because the program to reduce absent students had been in place for a year, the principal decided to **evaluate** if it had been successful.

4. Jack and Andrea were **honest** with their server at dinner and let him know he forgotten to bring them their bill.

5. After going for a dip in the ice cold water, Rebecca's arms and legs felt completely **numb** and she had a hard time moving.

How would you define the following?

construct: _____

_____

daughter: _____

_____

evaluated: _____

_____

CONTINUED >>

honest: _____

_____

numb: _____

_____

Check your answers against the correct definitions in the back of the book. Then return to complete the next two activities.

KEEP IT CLOZE

Fill in the following blanks based on your new knowledge of the word definitions.

1. I was so scared during the horror movie, my entire body felt _____.

2. My friend Ella has a _____ that looks and acts exactly like her.

3. If I'm being **honest**, my favorite food to eat is _____.

4. Meghan was hired to **construct** the _____ for the school.

5. When I had to _____ Andrea's dog on how well he performed, I was scared she would be upset because he did horribly.

ASK AND ANSWERED

To strengthen your verbal familiarity with each word, ask a parent, sibling, or friend each of these questions.

1. If you were an architect, what kinds of buildings would you **construct**?

2. Is it hard to be **honest** with your friends sometimes?

3. Have you ever fallen asleep and woken up to a **numb** hand or arm?

4. What do you think makes a nice son or **daughter**?

5. Would you find it hard to **evaluate** your best friend on something?

LESSON 32

Try to determine each word's meaning by how it is used in each sentence.

1. Many of my friends have **ambitions** to move away from home and go to college in another state.

2. Jack is often **anxious** during a sports game if his favorite team is losing.

3. Whenever I go to the doctor, I make sure to ask them a lot of questions because if they write information down it's often **illegible** and difficult to read when I get home.

4. Our dog Brae was **oblivious** to the little bunny in our yard and continued to nap by the window.

5. During the season, Maclain was an **essential** part of the team because nobody could swim the backstroke as quickly as she could.

How would you define the following?

ambitions: _____

_____

anxious: _____

_____

illegible: _____

_____

oblivious: _____

_____

essential: _____

_____

Check your answers against the correct definitions in the back of the book.
Then return to complete the next two activities.

DIGGING FOR ROOTS

Complete the exercise based on the original roots you've learned for
each word.

Word parts often change the meaning of the word. Check out the
following examples and then think of your own words with that same
word part. Then write the definition of your three new words.

-ible: able to be

> *illegible* → *not able to be read*
> *accessible* → *able to be accessed*

_____ → _____

_____ → _____

_____ → _____

CONTINUED >>

SAME THING, DIFFERENT WORD

Using the vocabulary words from this lesson, find the synonym for each of the following words.

1. desire → _____

2. fundamental → _____

3. unclear → _____

4. inattentive → _____

5. distressed → _____

LESSON 33

Try to determine each word's meaning by how it is used in each sentence.

1. I pledged my **allegiance** to our choir last year. I won't do any other activity that takes time away from them.

2. Andi was nervous that showing her artwork at the art show would **diminish** the value of her favorite piece.

3. It was a high **priority** for Colleen to find pizza for dinner, and quickly! Everyone was so hungry.

4. Many schools have a dress code that **requires** students to dress a certain way.

5. One time Kevin decided to **violate** his school's dress code and got a week's worth of detention. He will never do that again!

How would you define the following?

allegiance: _____

_____

diminish: _____

_____

priority: _____

_____

require: _____

_____

CONTINUED >>

violate: _____

_____

Check your answers against the correct definitions in the back of the book. Then return to complete the next two activities.

OPPOSING VIEWS

Using the vocabulary words from this lesson, find the antonym for each of the following words.

1. comply → _____

2. unimportant → _____

3. disloyal → _____

4. expand → _____

5. not want → _____

CATEGORICALLY THINKING

Find the vocabulary word that best belongs with each group of words.

Vocabulary Word → _____
1. dwindle   2. reduce   3. wane

Vocabulary Word → _____
1. faithfulness   2. obedience   3. obligation

Vocabulary Word → _____
1. demand   2. expect   3. request

Vocabulary Word → _____
1. breach   2. disobey   3. offend

Vocabulary Word → _____
1. rank   2. precedence   3. arrangement

LESSON 34

Try to determine each word's meaning by how it is used in each sentence.

1. I was so nervous walking into my new school. Luckily, I knew someone from my softball team so I had an **ally** right away!

2. When I'm with my dad, I always try to **avoid** running into my friends because he can be so embarrassing!

3. After Trinity hurt my feelings, I knew that I needed to talk with her about it and **elaborate** on the details so she wouldn't do it again.

4. Walking on the beach, the taste of the salt is almost **tangible**.

5. The **repetition** of water dripping into the sink from the leaky faucet all night long nearly drove me up the wall!

How would you define the following?

ally: _____

_____

avoid: _____

_____

elaborate: _____

_____

tangible: _____

_____

repetition: _____

_____

Check your answers against the correct definitions in the back of the book. Then return to complete the next two activities.

KEEP IT CLOZE

Fill in the following blanks based on your new knowledge of the word definitions.

1. I try hard to **avoid** continuing bad habits, such as _____.

2. Although I think e-readers are great, sometimes I like real books because they give me something _____ to hold.

3. My best **ally** is _____ because they are always there for me.

4. I had to ask my friend Emma to _____ on the recipe so I would know the exact measurement for each ingredient.

5. The _____ of the laundry pile is nonstop.

CONTINUED >>

CATEGORICALLY THINKING

Find the vocabulary word that best belongs with each group of words.

Vocabulary Word → _____

1. develop   2. clarify   3. discuss

Vocabulary Word → _____

1. recurrence   2. reiteration   3. repeat

Vocabulary Word → _____

1. avert   2. escape   3. shun

Vocabulary Word → _____

1. touchable   2. palpable   3. manifest

Vocabulary Word → _____

1. colleague   2. friend   3. associate

LESSON 35

Try to determine each word's meaning by how it is used in each sentence.

1. I hope I'll have **ample** time to present my science fair experiment. I learned so much and I can't wait to share all of the details!

2. My mom was ready to **anticipate** the worst, but the visit to the dentist went surprisingly well.

3. When I finally received a **response** from my teacher about my question, it was too late to turn everything in to him.

4. Some nights it's easy to **soothe** my little brother. Other nights he'll scream for hours and hours, keeping everyone awake.

5. James always has the most fun and **unique** shoes that he buys while traveling. Nobody else ever has a similar pair.

How would you define the following?

ample: _____

_____

anticipate: _____

_____

response: _____

_____

CONTINUED >>

soothe: _____

_____

unique: _____

_____

Check your answers against the correct definitions in the back of the book. Then return to complete the next two activities.

ASK AND ANSWERED

To strengthen your verbal familiarity with each word, ask a parent, sibling, or friend each of these questions.

1. What is a **unique** quality that makes you special?

2. Do you feel like you have **ample** time during the day? Why or why not?

3. How would you **soothe** an upset pet?

4. Do you **anticipate** any issues in the next presidential election?

5. Were your **responses** to these questions truthful?

SAME THING, DIFFERENT WORD

Using the vocabulary words from this lesson, find the synonym for each of the following words.

1. bountiful → _____

2. feedback → _____

3. uncommon → _____

4. pacify → _____

5. foresee → _____

LESSON 36

Try to determine each word's meaning by how it is used in each sentence.

1.   Because our new cat wasn't sure about our family yet, she was **apprehensive** about all the attention we gave her.

2.   After donating blood, the nurse told me to remain **horizontal** on the bed until I didn't feel faint anymore.

3.   It's important to take **frequent** breaks during the day and stretch to prevent stiff muscles.

4.   I was so excited to **proceed** with our party plans and start pulling everything together.

5.   It's only **logical** that we would take the back roads to school in the morning; they're not as busy.

How would you define the following?

apprehensive: _____

_____

horizontal: _____

_____

frequent: _____

_____

proceed: _____

_____

logical: _____

_____

Check your answers against the correct definitions in the back of the book. Then return to complete the next two activities.

DIGGING FOR ROOTS

Complete the exercise based on the original roots you've learned for each word.

Word parts often change the meaning of the word. Check out the following examples and then think of your own words with that same word part. Then write the definition of your two new words.

-al: means the subject has that characteristic

   horizontal → *being situated similar to the horizon*
   logical → *having logic*

_____ → _____

_____ → _____

CONTINUED >>

36

OPPOSING VIEWS

Using the vocabulary words from this lesson, find the antonym for each of the following words.

1. upright → _____

2. confident → _____

3. foolish → _____

4. cease → _____

5. inconstant → _____

PRONUNCIATION GUIDE

a	cat, flap		**ō**	lobe, snow
ā	page, face		**ô**	lord, board
ä	far		**oi**	boy, soil
b	bar, cab		**ou**	cow, doubt
CH	check, catch		**o͝o**	full, book
d	doll, bad		**o͞o**	ghoul, boo
e	pet, best		**p**	part, trap
ē	eat, bee		**r**	run, star
er	germ, earn		**s**	sell, mess
f	fear, leaf		**SH**	bash, flush
g	grow, leg		**t**	tire, great
h	her, hand		**TH**	thump, path
i	itch, tin		**ϴ**	them, breathe
ī	idle, wire		**v**	vest, cove
j	joke, giraffe		**w**	word, wilt
k	key, rock		**y**	yum, yell
l	low, ball		**z**	zoo, graze
m	man, ram		**ZH**	measure, vision
n	nose, run		**ə**	as in the *a* in *alert* or the *e* in *taken*
NG	sing, wrong			
o	lock, dot			

DEFINITIONS

LESSON 1 DEFINITIONS

abandon [*uh*-**ban**-d*uh*n]

verb—to give up control over someone or something

Matthew had to abandon his idea of hamburgers for dinner when his sister decided she wanted to be vegetarian.

verb—to leave without wanting to ever return

They abandoned their walk through the woods when they heard a scary noise ahead of them.

(first used in the late 1300s; derived from the French word *abandoner* meaning "surrender, give freely")

genuine [**jen**-yoo-in]

adjective—possessing a great character or quality; kind and honest

Rhea is an extremely genuine person, always willing to help and support you.

(first recorded in the 1600s; from the Latin word *genuinus* meaning "innate, natural")

irrigate [**ir**-i-geyt]

verb—to supply land with water by artificial means

The farmers had to irrigate their fields so water could flow to the crops.

verb—to flush a body part with water

The doctor irrigated the wound.

(first recorded in the 1610s; from the Latin word *irrigatus* meaning "wet, flood, nourish with water")

navigate [**nav**-i-geyt]

verb—to steer and move on a route by land, sea, or air

We chose to navigate the plane through the storm, even though it would be dangerous.

(first used in the 1580s; from the Latin word *navigare* meaning "to sail, sail over, go by sea, steer a ship")

reinforce [**ree**-in-fawrs]

verb—to strengthen something by adding support

Kalico wanted to reinforce her argument, so she added more stories to make it even stronger.

(first used in the 1600s; from the prefix *re-* meaning "again" and the word *enforce* meaning "exert force, compel; make stronger")

LESSON 2 DEFINITIONS

dangerous [**deyn**-jer-*uh*s]

adjective—something full of risk and involving possible harm

The walk through the dark woods was dangerous, but it was the only way to get to grandmother's house.

(first used in the 1200s; from the Old French word *dangereus* meaning "threatening, difficult")

discretion [**dih**-skresh-*uh*n]

noun—freedom to choose or act as you like

It's up to the teacher's discretion to decide what we learn next.

(first recorded in the 1300s; from the Middle English word *discrecioun* meaning "rational perception, good judgment")

chronological [kroon-l-**oj**-i-k*uh*l]

adjective—events arranged in the order of time

I flipped through the book and was excited to see what it was written in chronological order, starting with the earlier events and moving on to current events.

(first used in 1614; from the word *chronology*, meaning "the science of time," and the suffix *-ical*)

communication [k*uh*-myoon-ni-**key**-sh*uh*n]

noun—a process where information is exchanged between individuals

Our communication was so great that we barely had to talk anymore. We could communicate with just a glance at each other.

noun—a verbal or written message

The communication between troops was important because it made sure everyone was on the same page during the war.

(first recorded in the late 1300s; from the Latin word *communicationem*)

government [**guhv**-ern-m*uh*nt]

noun—the political direction and control over a community's citizens

I love learning about our government and how they develop laws.

(first recorded in the late 1300s; from the Old French word *governement* meaning "control, direction, administration")

LESSON 3 DEFINITIONS

accommodate [*uh*-**kom**-*uh*-deyt]

verb—to provide someone or something with a need or favor

I tried to accommodate the needs of my picky eaters, but it was hard to find something they liked!

(first recorded in the 1530s; from the Latin word *accomodatus* meaning "suitable, fit, appropriate to")

exaggerate [ig-**zaj**-*uh*-reyt]

verb—to magnify something way beyond the truth

My friend Tricia loves to exaggerate in order to make stories more dramatic.

(first recorded in the 1530s; from the Latin word *exaggeratus* meaning "heap up, pile, increase in significance")

invest [in-**vest**]

verb—to use money in order to make more money

I think I'll invest my money in baseball cards.

(first recorded in late 1300s; from the Latin word *investire* meaning "to clothe")

strategy [**strat**-i-jee]

noun—a plan or method for obtaining a specific goal

My favorite strategy for studying is to do a little bit every day.

(first recorded in the 1800s; from the Greek word *strategia* meaning "office or command of a general, generalship")

verdict [**vur**-dikt]

noun—the decision or judgment of a jury in a trial

The verdict was decided in record time.

(first recorded in the 1300s; from the Middle English word *verdit* meaning "something said truly")

calculate [**kal**-kyuh-leyt]

verb—to determine using mathematical processes

When I go grocery shopping, I try to calculate my total before the cash register.

(first recorded in the 1560s; from the Latin word *calculatus* meaning "pebble, small stone")

embarrass [em-**bar**-uhs]

verb—to make uncomfortable; to cause confusion and shame

My dog will embarrass me in front of my friends if he refuses to sit when I tell him to sit.

(first recorded in the 1600s; from the French word *embarrasser* meaning "to block, to obstruct")

heroic [hi-**roh**-ik]

adjective—a courageous quality; showing courage and daring

It was so heroic of the mom to run in and save the family's treasured photo albums.

(first recorded in the 1540s; from the Latin *heroicus* meaning "of a hero, heroic, mythical")

origin [**awr**-i-jin]

noun—the rise or beginning of something

The origin of a word can tell you a lot about the definition.

(first recorded in the 1400s; from the Middle English word *origine* meaning "beginning, source")

paraphrase [**par**-uh-freyz]

noun—a restatement of a text or passage giving the meaning in another form

I wanted my sister to read my favorite book, so I paraphrased the story for her, focusing on the more exciting parts.

(first recorded in the 1540s; from the Latin word *paraphrasis* meaning "a paraphrase")

benefit [**ben**-uh-fit]

noun—something that is good or produces an advantage

I don't have a pet of my own, but I benefit from my neighbor having an outdoor cat that loves to lie on our porch!

(first recorded in the late 1300; from the Late Middle English word *benefytt* meaning "good deed")

familiar [fuh-**mil**-yer]

noun—commonly or generally known or understood

I was already familiar with the material on our test, so I didn't need to study.

(first recorded in the 1300s; from the Latin word *familiaris* meaning "family")

humor [**hyoo**-mer]

noun—something that is designed to be comical or amusing

It's easy to find the humor in jokes on April Fool's Day.

(first recorded in the 1300s; from the Middle English word *humour*)

know [noh]

verb—to understand something as fact or truth

I would like to know what your favorite comic book is.

(recorded before 900; from the Middle English word *knowen* meaning "recognize, known")

source [sohrs]

noun—the beginning or place of origin

The source of my favorite books is my favorite author, J. K. Rowling.

(first recorded in the 1300s; from the Middle English word *sours* meaning "rise, to spring up")

LESSON 6 DEFINITIONS

dimension [dih-**men**-sh*uh*n]

noun—a measure in one direction

I found the dimensions of my bedroom so I could plan out my new furniture.

(first recorded in the late 1300s; from the late Middle English word *dimensioun* meaning "measured out")

dissatisfied [dis-**sat**-is-fahyd]

adjective—not satisfied or pleased

I was dissatisfied with my meal but I didn't want to be rude, so I ate small bites when they were watching.

(first recorded in the mid-1660s; from the Latin prefix *dis-*, meaning "negative," and the word *satisfy* meaning "needs")

encourage [en-**kur**-ij]

verb—to inspire with support, courage, or confidence

My friend Lisa is the first to encourage me when I am nervous or anxious about something.

(first recorded in the 1400s; from the late Middle English word *encoragen*; the prefix *en-*, meaning "to cause," and the word *courage*, meaning "bravery")

maximum [**mak**-s*uh*-muhm]

noun—the greatest quantity or amount possible

The maximum weight limit for our tree fort is 400 pounds.

(first recorded in the late 1700s; from the Latin word *magnus* meaning "great, large")

tentative [**ten**-t*uh*-tiv]

adjective—something that is uncertain or subject to change

Our schedule on Thanksgiving was tentative since my dad was on call and could have to leave any minute.

(first recorded in the 1580s; from the Medieval Latin word *tentativus*, variant of *temptare*, meaning "to feel, to test, try")

LESSON 7 DEFINITIONS

democracy [dih-**mok**-r*uh*-see]

noun—a form of government by the people, ruled by the majority

Voting is part of being in a democracy.

(first recorded in the mid-1500s; from the Latin word *democratia*, meaning "popular government")

forecast [**fawr**-kast]

verb—to predict some future occurrence

When I wake up in the morning, I check the daily weather forecast.

(first recorded in the 1400s; from the Middle English word *forecasten* meaning "to plan beforehand, prepare")

guard [gahrd]

verb—to protect or keep safe from harm

Our dog loves to guard the front door and make sure we're safe.

(first recorded in the 1400s; from the French word *garder* meaning "watch over, protect")

hostile [**hos**-tl]

adjective—characteristic of an enemy

The swarm of bees was extremely hostile.

(first recorded in the 1500s; from the Latin word *hostilis* meaning "enemy")

museum [myoo-**zee**-uhm]

noun—a building devoted to works of art or objects of value

An afternoon at the museum is a great way to spend some time.

(first recorded in the 1600s; from the Latin word *museum* meaning "shrine of the Muses")

LESSON 8 DEFINITIONS

equation [ih-**kwey**-zhuhn]

noun—the act or process of making equal or equating

I love solving a tough equation.

(first recorded in the late 1300s; from the Latin word *aequation* meaning "make equal, equalization")

extensive [ik-**sten**-siv]

adjective—the degree to which a thing extends; having considerable extent

I have an extensive collection of warm, fuzzy socks.

(first recorded in the early 1600s; from the Late Latin word *extensivus* meaning "extend, spread")

generous [**jen**-er-uhs]

adjective—willing to give or share liberally

It's important to be generous with your time when you can.

(first recorded in the 1580s; from the Middle French word *genereux* meaning "of noble birth, magnanimous")

gradual [**graj** oo-uhl]

adjective—altering little by little

My hunger was gradual at first and then got much worse.

(first recorded in the early 1400s; from the Medieval Latin word *gradualis* pertaining to steps)

guilty [**gil**-tee]

adjective—responsible for committing an offense or crime

My little sister was guilty of stealing an extra piece of candy after dinner.

(first recorded before 1100; from the Old English word *gyltig* meaning "offending, criminal")

LESSON 9 DEFINITIONS

abolish [uh-**bol**-ish]

verb—to put an end to

Outdated rules should be abolished.

(first recorded in mid-1400s; from the Latin word *abolere* meaning "put an end to, destroy")

analyze [**an** l-ahyz]

verb—to study or examine critically

I love to analyze the needs of my friends and try to find them the perfect gift.

(first recorded in the late 1500s; from the French word *analyser*)

behavior [bih-**heyv**-yer]

noun—the way in which someone conducts oneself

My cat's behavior was not very nice.

(first recorded in the late 1400s; from the Middle English word *behavoure*)

citizen [sit-uh-zuhn]

noun—an inhabitant of a state or nation

I'm proud to be a citizen of my country.

(first recorded in the early 1300s; from the Anglo-French word *citezein* meaning "city-dweller, town-dweller")

persuade [per-**sweyd**]

verb—to move by argument or course of action

I'm going to persuade my parents to let me choose dinner tonight!

(first recorded in the early 1500s; from the Latin word *persuadere* meaning "to bring over by talking")

LESSON 10 DEFINITIONS

accomplish [*uh*-**kom**-plish]

verb—to carry out a goal or bring to completion

I hope I can accomplish all my chores before my friends get here.

(first recorded in the late 1300s; from the Latin word *complere* meaning "to fill up, complete")

approximate [*uh*-**prok**-s*uh*-mit]

adjective—nearly correct or exact; close to meeting a condition, goal, or standard

Let's find an approximate date for our holiday party.

(first recorded in the from the Late Latin word *approximatus* meaning "drawn near to, come near to")

exhaust [ig-**zawst**]

verb—to drain of strength or tire completely

I want to exhaust all of my options before I resort to fast food.

(first recorded in the 1500s; from the Latin word *exhaustus* meaning "to draw out, use up, empty")

quality [**kwol**-i-tee]

noun—an essential characteristic

Julie's kindness is her best quality.

(first recorded in the 1300s; from the Latin word *qualitatem* meaning "of what kind")

swarm [swawrm]

verb—to move about in great numbers

The swarm of bees is scary to me!

(used before 1100; from the Middle English word *swearm* meaning "multitude")

LESSON 11 DEFINITIONS

accumulate [*uh*-**kyoo**-my*uh*-leyt]

verb—to gather or pile up

I will accumulate a bunch of leaves to draw pictures of.

(first recorded in the 1520s; from the Latin word *accumulatus* meaning "heaped up, amass")

arid [**ar**-id]

adjective—extremely dry

The air here is arid.

(first recorded in the 1650s; from the Latin word *arere* meaning "to be dry")

cease [sees]

verb—to stop or discontinue

I would love to cease the discussion about my new purple hair. I love it!

(first recorded in the 1300s; from the Latin word *cessare* meaning "to cease, to leave off")

courage [**kur**-ij]

noun—mental or moral strength

It takes courage to stand up to a bully.

(first recorded in the 1300s; from the Old French word *corage* meaning "heart")

remain [ri-**meyn**]

verb—to continue in the same state

I think our holiday traditions will remain intact, even if we are not at our house.

(first recorded in the 1300s; from the Latin word *remanere* meaning "to stay behind")

LESSON 12 DEFINITIONS

compose [k*uh*m-**pohz**]

verb—to form by putting together

I want to compose a beautiful piece of music.

(first recorded in the 1400s; from the Old French word *composer* meaning "put together, compound")

declare [dih-**klair**]
verb—to announce officially

Later today the class president will declare that we are going to get out of school 10 minutes early.

(first recorded in the 1300s; from the Middle English word *declaren* meaning "explain, make clear")

obedient [oh-**bee**-dee-*uh*nt]
adjective—agreeable to a command or request

The teacher asked her students to be obedient so they could participate in a fun class activity.

(first recorded in the 1200s; from the Old French word *obedient* meaning "to obey")

oppose [*uh*-**pohz**]
verb—to act against

My cat is opposed to eating any food that isn't fresh.

(first recorded in the 1300s; from the Middle English word *opposen* meaning "speak or act against, examine")

unanimous [yoo-**nah**-nuh-m*uh*s]
adjective—complete agreement

The neighborhood made the unanimous decision to put streetlights in so it wouldn't be so hard to see at night.

(first recorded in the 1620s; from the Latin words *unus*, meaning "one," and *animus*, meaning "mind, spirit")

LESSON 13 DEFINITIONS

ancient [**eyn**-sh*uh*nt]
adjective—something that has been in existence for many years

The chest in our attic is ancient.

(first recorded in the 1300s; from the Middle English word *auncyen* meaning "very old")

artifact [**ahr**-t*uh*-fakt]
noun—a simple object made by humans

Cave dwellers left behind many artifacts that tell us about their lives.

(first recorded in the 1800s; from the Latin phrase *arte factum* meaning "made with skill")

curious [**kyoor**-ee-*uh*s]
adjective—excited and eager to learn

I am extremely curious about outer space.

(first recorded in the early 1300s; from the Latin word *curiosus* meaning "careful, inquisitive")

gigantic [jahy-**gan**-tik]
adjective—extremely large or huge

Compared to a mouse, elephants are gigantic.

(first recorded in the early 1600s; from the Latin word *gigas* meaning "giant")

manipulate [muh-**nip**-y*uh*-leyt]
verb—to manage or influence someone

It's always easy to manipulate my little sister into helping me with my chores.

(first recorded in the early 1800s; from the Latin word *manipulus* meaning "hand")

LESSON 14 DEFINITIONS

consistent [k*uh*n-**sis**-t*uh*nt]
adjective—acting in the same way over time

I think it's important to take consistent showers every week.

(first recorded in the late 1500s; from the Latin word *consistent* meaning "to stand firm")

impatient [im-**pey**-shuhnt]

adjective—restless or short of temper

My little brother is extremely impatient whenever we go out to eat.

(first recorded in the late 1400s; from the Middle English word *impacient*)

massive [**mas**-iv]

adjective—forming an extremely large mass

The new bridge is massive!

(first recorded in the early 1400s; from the late Middle English word *massif* meaning "bulky, solid")

superior [suh-**peer**-ee-er]

adjective—higher up in importance

Vegetable pizza is superior to pepperoni pizza.

(first recorded in the late 1300s; from the Latin word *super* meaning "over, above")

vertical [**vur**-ti-kuhl]

adjective—a line or plane that goes up and down

I climbed up the vertical wall with the help of a ladder.

(first recorded in the 1550s; from the Late Latin word *verticalis* meaning "overhead")

LESSON 15 DEFINITIONS

consequence [**kon**-si-kwens]

noun—the result of something happening

When I showed up late to school, my consequence was getting detention from our principal.

(first recorded in the 1300s; from the Latin word *consequentia* meaning "to follow after")

drastic [**dras**-tik]

adjective—acting rapidly; extreme in action

I had to resort to drastic measures when I saw a cat stuck in a small pool of water.

(first recorded in the 1690s; from the Greek word *drastikos* meaning "active, effective, violent")

mention [**men**-shuhn]

verb—to refer to someone or something in a casual manner

I heard someone mention my name.

(first recorded in the 1300s; from the Latin word *mention* meaning "a calling to mind")

rhythm [**rith**-uhm]

noun—movement with uniform or patterned recurrence

My favorite songs have a steady rhythm.

(first recorded in the mid-1500s; from the Latin word *rhythmus* meaning "movement in time")

service [**sur**-vis]

noun—a helpful activity or job

I spent my weekend in service to individuals experiencing homelessness.

(first recorded in the 1100s; from the Latin word *servitium* meaning "servitude")

LESSON 16 DEFINITIONS

contribute [kuhn-**trib**-yoot]

verb—to give

Megan will contribute green bean casserole to our dinner on Sunday.

(first recorded in the early 1520s; from the Latin word *contributes* meaning "add, unite, to bring together")

moreover [mawr-**oh**-ver]

adverb—in addition to what has been said

In the winter I want to travel somewhere warm, moreover, so I can get some sun on my face.

(first recorded in the 1400s; from the Middle English phrase *more over* meaning "there is more to say")

narrate [**nar**-eyt]
    verb—to tell a story

    My baby brother loves to narrate his books.

    (first recorded in 1656; from the Latin word *narratus* meaning "to tell, to relate")

quest [kwest]
    noun—a search to find something

    I was on a quest to find the perfect dress for our school dance.

    (first recorded in the 1300s; from the Middle English word *queste* meaning "search, pursuit")

squeeze [skweez]
    verb—to exert pressure forcibly

    I had to squeeze the lemon to get juice out of it.

    (first recorded in the 1600s; possibly from the Old English word *cwysan* meaning "to squeeze, to crush")

LESSON 17 DEFINITIONS

adapt [*uh* **dapt**]
    verb—to make adjustments

    I was hoping to cook breakfast early, but I had to adapt when I realized our power was out and wouldn't be able to use our toaster and oven.

    (first recorded in the 1400s; from the Latin word *adaptare* meaning "to fit, adjust")

peculiar [pi-**kyool**-yer]
    adjective—strange or odd

    The shape of the tree in our front yard is extremely peculiar.

    (first recorded in the 1400s; from the Latin word *peculiaris* meaning "as one's own")

quote [kwoht]
    verb—to repeat from a book, speech, or something else while providing credit to the author

My dad loves to quote old movies constantly.

(first recorded in the from the Medieval Latin word *quotare* meaning "to divide into chapters, distinguish by numbers")

tension [**ten**-sh*uh*n]
    noun—mental or physical strain, anxiety, or excitement

    I could feel the tension in my back from bending over and writing all afternoon.

    (first recorded in the 1530s; from the Latin word *tension* meaning "process of drawing tight, a stretching")

variable [**vair**-ee-*uh*-b*uh*l]
    adjective—able to change; changeable

    The new light bulbs offer variable colors.

    (first recorded in the 1300s; from the late Middle English word *variabilis* meaning "changeable")

LESSON 18 DEFINITIONS

monotonous [m*uh*-**not**-n-*uh*s]
    adjective—lacking in variety

    I find the lunch options at school to be awfully monotonous.

    (first recorded in the late 1700s; from the Late Greek word *monotonos* meaning "of one tone")

transfer [trans-**fur**]
    verb—to move from one place to another

    I like to transfer our Halloween decorations from one room to another each year.

    (first recorded in the 1300s; from the Latin word *transferre* meaning "bear across, to carry")

transport [trans-**pawrt**]
    verb—to carry or move from one place to another

    I was excited to transport my favorite books to our new house.

(first recorded in the 1300s; from the Latin word *transportare* meaning "to carry across, convey")

unruly [uhn-**roo**-lee]

adjective—not confirming to rule

My friend's little brother is so unruly, I refuse to babysit him.

(first recorded in the 1400s; from the Middle English word *unruely* meaning "not ameanable to rule")

vacate [**vey**-keyt]

verb—to give up possession

At the end of the day, we have to vacate our favorite classroom so the teachers can have a meeting.

(first recorded in the 1640s; from the Latin word *vacatus* meaning "to annul, to be empty")

LESSON 19 DEFINITIONS

adequate [**ad**-i-kwit]

adjective—sufficient for a specific requirement

I think one blanket will be adequate for this cool night.

(first recorded in the 1610s; from the Latin word *adaequatus* meaning "equalized")

appropriate [*uh*-**prop**-pree-it]

adjective—suitable or fitting for a specific purpose

Can you help me find an appropriate book to read?

(first recorded in the 1400s; from the late Latin word *appropriates* meaning "made one's own")

recount [ri-**kount**]

verb—to tell in detail

I will recount my favorite part of the day so my parents understand why I'm so excited.

(first recorded in the 1400s; from the late Middle English word *recounter* meaning "to tell or count")

specific [spi-**sif**-ik]

adjective—having a special distinction

The tree I'm looking for has a specific set of oddly shaped branches.

(first recorded in the 1630s; from the Late Latin word *specificus* meaning "constituting a kind or sort")

trait [treyt]

noun—a distinguishing characteristic

My dog has the silliest trait of sitting on his back legs and raising his front legs.

(first recorded in the 1400s; from the Latin word *tractus* meaning "drawing, dragging")

LESSON 20 DEFINITIONS

foundation [foun-**dey**-sh*uh*n]

noun—a basis upon which something stands

The foundation of our house is sturdy and strong.

(first recorded in the late 1300s; from the Latin word *fundation* meaning "to lay a base for")

outstanding [out-**stan**-ding]

adjective—standing out; marked by excellence

I found an outstanding recipe for apple pie!

(first recorded in the 1610s; from the word *out* and the word *standing*, meaning "upright")

selection [si-**lek**-sh*uh*n]

noun—the process of choosing someone or something

The football team's music selection was surprising but I liked it.

(first recorded in the 1620s; from the Latin word *selectio* meaning "a choosing out, choice")

substitute [**suhb**-sti-toot]

noun—a person or thing serving in place of another

I don't like pepperoni so I always substitute mushrooms for it on my pizzas.

(first recorded in the 1400s; from the Latin word *substituere* meaning "to put in place of")

treacherous [**trech**-er-*uh*s]

adjective—dangerous or hazardous

The roads were treacherous after the snow storm.

adjective—deceptive or untrustworthy

I knew that lying was a treacherous act of betrayal, but I didn't know what else to do.

(first recorded in the 1300s; from the Middle English word *treacherous* meaning "deceiver")

LESSON 21 DEFINITIONS

anguish [**ang**-gwish]

noun—extreme pain or distress

I was in great anguish after falling out of the tree and landing on a rock.

(first recorded in the 1200s; from Anglo-French word *anguisse* meaning "choking sensation, distress")

business [**biz**-nis]

noun—an occupation or profession

My favorite business is the local coffee shop by my house.

(first recorded before 950; from the Old English world *bisygnesse* meaning "busy ness")

gist [jist]

noun—the main point

Can you tell me the gist of what happened?

(first recorded in 1711; from the Anglo-French word *gist* meaning "it lies in, it lies")

insist [in-**sist**]

verb—to be firm and resolute about a matter

I insist that you let me ride my bike home with you.

(first recorded in the 1580s; from the Latin word *insistere* meaning "to stand still on, dwell upon, take a stand")

revolt [ri-**vohlt**]

verb—to break away from

After learning that they would have more homework over the holidays, students decided to revolt and not do their homework.

(first recorded in the mid-1550s; from the Middle French word *revolter* meaning "to turn around, overthrow")

LESSON 22 DEFINITIONS

cough [kawf]

verb—to clear your lungs with a harsh noise

Whenever I walk out into cold air, I cough really loudly.

(first recorded in the 1400s; from the German word *keuchen* meaning "to wheeze, breathe heavily")

factor [**fak**-ter]

noun—an element contributing to a situation

We have to factor in my younger brother's naptime when we make plans during the summer.

(first recorded in the 1400s; from the Latin work *facere* meaning "to make")

height [hahyt]

noun—distance upward

I love rock climbing; the height does not scare me.

(first recorded before 900; from the Old English word *hiehtho* meaning "high, highest part")

toxic [**tok**-sik]

adjective—acting as or having the effect of a poison

After sitting in the car for a week, the juice was pretty much toxic.

(first recorded in the 1660s; from the Late Latin word *toxicus* meaning "poisonous")

viewpoint [**vyoo**-point]

noun—a position or perspective from which something is considered

From my viewpoint, it's okay to fail when you're trying to learn something new.

(first recorded in the 1850s; alteration of *point of view*)

LESSON 23 DEFINITIONS

conserve [kuhn-**surv**]

verb—to use or manage wisely

I try to conserve water in our house by turning the faucet off in between dishes I'm washing.

(first recorded in the 1300s; from the Latin word *conservare* meaning "to save")

knack [nak]

noun—a special skill or talent

My mom has a knack for knowing when I am lying.

(first recorded in the 1300s; from the Middle English word *knak*)

lofty [**lawf**-tee]

adjective—elevated in character or status

My goal to read 60 books in a year is lofty, but I think I can accomplish it.

(first recorded in the 1400s; late Middle English word *loft* meaning "elevated")

negotiate [ni-**goh**-shee-yet]

verb—to discuss with another; to arrive at an agreement of something

I am hoping to negotiate a later curfew with my parents.

(first recorded in the 1590s; from the Latin word *negotiatus* meaning "to trade")

philosophy [fi-**los**-uh-fee]

noun—a pursuit of knowledge and wisdom

It is my philosophy that people should not litter.

A philosopher is one who practices philosophy

(first recorded in the 1300s; from the Middle English word *philosophie* meaning "philosophy, knowledge")

LESSON 24 DEFINITIONS

effective [ih-**fek**-tiv]

adjective—producing a desired effect

I think the most effective form of saving money is putting it somewhere you cannot see it.

(first recorded in the 1300s; from the Latin word *effectivus* meaning "practical, productive")

expression [ik-**spresh**-uhn]

noun—the act or process of sharing words

Judging by their expression, I'm not sure they liked the present.

(first recorded in the early 1400s; from the Latin word *expression* meaning "pressing out")

ferocious [fuh-**roh**-shuhs]

adjective—savagely fierce; extreme or intense

My cat is ferocious.

(first recorded in the 1640s; from the Latin stem *feroc-* meaning "savage")

influence [**in**-floo-uhns]

noun—the power or capacity to cause an effect

My soccer coach can influence how much we work out and what type of diet we have during our season so that we can stay at our best.

(first recorded in the 1300s; from the Latin word *influere* meaning "to flow into, stream in")

objective [uhb-**jek**-tiv]

noun—something that one's actions are intended to attain

Their objective was to get to the other yard, so they climbed the fence and jumped over.

(first recorded in the 1600s; from the Medieval Latin word *objectivus* meaning "considered in relation to its purpose")

LESSON 25 DEFINITIONS

alarming [uh-**lahr**-ming]

adjective—causing alarm or fear

The car horn was alarming.

(first recorded in the mid-1600s)

pleasant [**plez**-uhnt]

adjective—having qualities that are agreeable or enjoyable

The weather is so pleasant during the spring.

(first recorded in the 1300s; from the Middle English word *plesaunt* meaning "to please")

realistic [ree-uh-**lis**-tik]

adjective—based on what is real or practical

I believe it is not realistic to read 10 chapter books in one day.

(first recorded in 1829; from the word *reaist*)

thesis [**thee**-sis]

noun—a proposition stated or put forward for consideration

My thesis is that English can be learned best by reading.

(first recorded in the 1300s; from the Greek word *thesis* meaning "a setting down")

vibrant [**vahy**-bruh-nt]

adjective—energetic; vital; vigorous

The colors of the rainbow were vibrant.

(first recorded in the 1550s; from the Latin word *vibrare* meaning "to shake, move to and fro")

LESSON 26 DEFINITIONS

awkward [**awk**-werd]

adjective—lacking social graces, grace, or ease in movement

My friend can be very awkward whenever she meets parents.

(first recorded in the early 1500s; from the Middle English word *awke*, meaning "back-handed," and the suffix *weard*)

backward [**bak**-werd]

adverb—toward the back

I think it's fun to sit backward sometimes.

(first recorded in the 1300s; from the Old English word *babkward*)

balance [**bal**-uhns]

noun—equal distribution of weight or amount

I love to balance on top of the slide at home.

(first recorded in the 1200s; from the Late Latin word *bilanx* meaning "scale, having two pans")

ridiculous [ri-**dik**-*yuh-luh*s]

adjective—absurd and laughable

I think it is ridiculous that we have to write a 10-page paper.

(first recorded in the from the late Latin word *ridiculosus* meaning "laughable")

predict [pri-**dikt**]

verb—to tell in advance

Many people can predict the weather just by looking at the sky.

(first recorded in the early 1600s; from the Latin word *praedictus* meaning "foretell, advise")

LESSON 27 DEFINITIONS

adjacent [*uh*-**jey**-*suh*nt]

adjective—just before, after, or facing

We walked over to the adjacent street.

(first recorded in the early 1400s; from the Latin word *adjacent* meaning "to adjoin")

catastrophe [*kuh*-**tas**-*truh*-fee]

noun—a sudden disaster, misfortune, or failure

The tree falling on their house during the hurricane was a catastrophe.

(first recorded in the mid-1500s; from the Greek word *katastrophe* meaning "an overturning")

scarce [skairs]

adjective—insufficient to satisfy the need

Food was scarce during the holidays.

adjective—intentionally absent

The mice made themselves scarce when they knew the cat was inside too.

(first recorded in the 1300s; from the Middle English word *scars* meaning "plucked out")

solution [*suh*-**loo**-*shuhn*]

noun—the act of solving a problem or question

I think the perfect solution for figuring out dinner is ordering pizza.

(first recorded in the 1300s; from the Middle English word *solucion* meaning "explanation")

tremble [**trem**-*buh*l]

verb—to shake in fear, excitement, or cold

I began to tremble as the football game got more and more exciting!

(first recorded in the 1300s; from the Anglo-French word *trembler* meaning "tremble, fear")

LESSON 28 DEFINITIONS

capacity [*kuh*-**pas**-i-tee]

noun—the potential for holding or storing

The swimming pool has reached its capacity of people.

noun—the ability to perform

Their capacity to dance is impressive.

(first recorded in the 1400s; from the late Middle English word *capacite* meaning "ability to hold")

deconstruct [**dee**-*kuh*-n-**struhkt**]

verb—to break down into parts

It won't take long to deconstruct the run-down house.

(first recorded in 1973; formation of the word *deconstruction*)

devote [dih-**voht**]

verb—to concentrate on a particular pursuit

I devote 20 hours a week to learning to play the piano.

(first recorded in 1580; from the Latin word *devotus* meaning "vowed")

extend [ik-**stend**]

verb—to stretch out

It was simple to extend the leash out to its full length.

(first recorded in the early 1300s; from the Middle English word *extenden* meaning "to stretch out")

retrieve [ri-**treev**]

verb—to bring back to a former state

I went inside to retrieve my keys that I had forgotten.

(first recorded in the early 1400s; from the late Middle English word *retreve* meaning "to find again")

LESSON 29 DEFINITIONS

announce [*uh*-**nouns**]

verb—to make known publicly or officially

I can't wait for them to announce the newest movie.

(first recorded in the 1500s; from the Old French word *anoncier* meaning "proclaim")

history [**his**-t*uh*-ree]

noun—an account of events that occurred in the past

The history of the Ancient Egyptians is amazing.

(first recorded in the late 1300s; from the Greek word *historia* meaning "learning, record")

immigrate [**im**-i-greyt]

verb—to come to a new country for permanent residence

My parents had to immigrate to Greece to find new jobs.

(first recorded in the 1620s; from the Latin word *immigratus* meaning "to move into")

similar [**sim**-*uh*-ler]

adjective—having characteristics in common

My best friend and I are very similar.

(first recorded in the 1610s; from the Latin word *similis* meaning "like")

suspense [s*uh*-**spens**]

noun—a state of mental excitement and uncertainty

The end of the book left us in suspense.

(first recorded in the early 1400s; from the Anglo-French word *suspens* meaning "abeyance")

LESSON 30 DEFINITIONS

civilization [siv-*uh*-luh-**zey**-sh*uh*n]

noun—any culture or society in a specific place

We were fascinated by the small civilization in South America that lives without electricity.

(first recorded in 1700s; from the French word *civilisation*)

conclusion [kuhn-**kloo**-zh*uh*n]

noun—the end or final part

The conclusion of the book was the best part.

(first recorded in the late 1300s; from the Latin word *conclusion* meaning "closed")

confident [**kon**-fi-d*uh*nt]

adjective—sure of oneself

I am confident that you will do great on today's test.

(first recorded in 1570; from the Latin word *confident* meaning "assured, reliant")

congruent [kun-**groo**-*uh*-nt]

adjective—being in agreement

My ideas were congruent with my mom's ideas.

(first recorded in the early 1400s; from the Latin word *congruent* meaning "to come together")

hypothesis [hi-**poth**-*uh*-sis]
noun—an assumption or concession made to draw out and test its consequences

The hypothesis is that plants will grow better with classical music playing.

(first recorded in the mid-1600s; from the Greek word *hypothesis* meaning "supposition")

LESSON 31 DEFINITIONS

construct [k*uh*n-**struhkt**]
verb—to build by putting parts together

Let's construct a house made with playing cards.

(first recorded in the 1660s; from the Latin word *constructus* meaning "accumulate, build")

daughter [**daw**-ter]
noun—a female descendant

I am my parent's only daughter.

(first recorded before 950; from the Middle English word *doughter*)

evaluate [ih-**val**-yoo-eyt]
verb—to determine the value of something

When I get new clothes, I like to evaluate their quality.

(first recorded in the mid-1800s; from the French word *evaluer*)

honest [**on**-ist]
adjective—free from deception

It's important to be honest even when you don't want to be.

(first recorded in the 1300s; from the Old French word *honeste* meaning "virtuous, decent")

numb [n*uh*m]
adjective—unable to feel

After sitting in on the cold bleachers for the entire game, my legs were numb.

(first recorded in the 1400s; from the late Middle English word *nome* meaning "seized")

LESSON 32 DEFINITIONS

ambition [am-**bish**-*uh*n]
noun—a desire for achievement

It's important to have ambition at school.

(first recorded in the 1300; from the Middle English word *ambicio* meaning "striving for favor")

anxious [**angk**-sh*uh*s]
adjective—uneasiness of the mind

I was anxious about getting sick again.

(first recorded in the early 1600s; from the Latin word *anxius* meaning "worried, uneasy")

essential [*uh*-**sen**-sh*uh*l]
adjective—completely necessary

It's essential that we include milkshakes in our summer celebration.

(first recorded in the 1300s; from the Middle English word *essencial* meaning "being, essence")

illegible [ih-**lej**-*uh*-buhl]
adjective—impossible or hard to read

My doctor's handwriting is often illegible.

(first recorded in the early 1600s; meaning "not legible")

oblivious [*uh*-**bliv**-ee-*uhs*]

adjective—unaware or forgetful

Our dog was completely oblivious that there was a cat sitting behind him, watching his every move.

(first recorded in the 1400s; from the Latin word *obliviosus* meaning "forgetful")

LESSON 33 DEFINITIONS

allegiance [*uh*-**lee**-j*uh*ns]

noun—loyalty to a person, group, or cause

I pledged my allegiance to my soccer club.

(first recorded in the 1300s; from the Middle English word *aligeaunce* "loyalty of liege-servant to one's lord")

diminish [dih-**min**-ish]

verb—to lessen or decrease

I don't want to diminish your ribbon, but I got a trophy.

(first recorded in the 1400s; from the Medieval Latin word *diminuere* meaning "to make smaller")

priority [prahy-**awr** i-tee]

noun—something given special attention

Writing your essay should take priority over getting dinner with your friend.

(first recorded in the 1300s; from the Old French word *priorite*)

require [ri-**kwahy**-*uhr*]

verb—to need something

During the hot summer, our yard requires extra water to survive.

(first recorded in the 1300; from the Middle English word *requiren*)

violate [**vahy**-*uh*-leyt]

verb—to disturb rudely

I hate when my friends violate my privacy by reading my text messages over my shoulder.

(first recorded in the early 1400s; from the Middle English word *violaten* meaning "to treat with violence")

LESSON 34 DEFINITIONS

ally [*uh*-**lahy**]

verb—to associate or connect by some mutual relationship

My best ally is my older brother.

(first recorded in the early 1300s; from the Middle English word *allien* meaning "to bind")

avoid [*uh*-**void**]

verb—to keep clear of

I hope to avoid getting sick this season.

(first recorded in the late 1300s; from the Middle English word *avoiden* meaning "to clear out")

elaborate [ih-**lab**-er-it]

adjective—worked out with great care

Please elaborate on how I make the green bean casserole.

(first recorded in the 1590s; from the Latin word *elaboratus* meaning "to labor")

repetition [rep-i-**tish**-*uh*n]

noun—the act of doing something again

I use repetition to study new vocabulary words.

(first recorded in the 1400s; from Middle English *repeticioun* meaning "to repeat")

tangible [**tan**-j*uh*-b*uh*l]

adjective—capable of being touched

My favorite birthday gifts are ones that are not tangible.

(first recorded in the 1580s; from the Late Latin *tangibilis* meaning "that may be touched")

LESSON 35 DEFINITIONS

ample [**am**-*puhl*]

adjective—more than adequate for the purpose or needs

We have ample snacks for the car ride.

(first recorded in the 1400s; from the Latin word *amplus* meaning "wide, large")

anticipate [an-**tis**-*uh*-peyt]

adjective—to expect or look forward to something

I anticipate that we'll be hungry later if we don't eat before the movie.

(first recorded in the 1560s; from the Latin word *anticipatus* meaning "taken before")

response [ri-**spahnns**]

noun—an answer or reply

His response made me laugh so hard.

(first recorded in the 1300s; from the Latin word *responsum* meaning "an answer")

soothe [soo*th*]

verb—to calm or comfort

When I am sick, nothing can soothe me.

(first recorded before 950; from the Middle English word *sothen* meaning "to verify")

unique [yoo-**neek**]

adjective—unlike anyone else in characteristics

Our school has a unique mascot.

(first recorded in the early 1600s; from the Latin word *unicus* meaning "only, sole")

LESSON 36 DEFINITIONS

apprehensive [ap-ri-**hen**-siv]

adjective—fearful about something that may happen

I am apprehensive about taking another honors class because they are so hard.

(first recorded in the 1300s; from the Medieval Latin word *apprehensivus*)

frequent [free-**kwuh**-nt]

adjective—happening at short intervals

We took frequent bathroom stops on our car ride and my dad was not happy.

(first recorded in the 1400s; from the late Middle English word *ample* meaning "profuse, often")

horizontal [hawr-*uh*-**zon**-tl]

adjective—flat or level to the ground

After the race, I was so tired that I lay horizontal on the ground.

(first recorded in the 1550s; from the Late Latin stem *horizont*)

logical [**loj**-i-k*uhl*]

adjective—reasonable, in accordance with logic

The most logical option is to eat dinner before we go to the football game.

(first recorded in the 1400s; from the Medieval Latin word *logicalis* meaning "pertaining to logic")

proceed [pr*uh*-**seed**]

verb—to carry on

Let's proceed with the math game.

(first recorded in the 1300s; from the Middle English *proceden* meaning "emanate from, result from")

ANSWER KEY

LESSON 1

KEEP IT CLOZE:

1. genuine
2. Answers will vary. Possible answers could be: a musical, my friend, the water tower
3. irrigate
4. Answers will vary. Possible answers could be: olives, corn, or any other food the child does not like
5. reinforce

ASK AND ANSWERED:
Answers will vary.

LESSON 2

DIGGING FOR ROOTS:
Answers will vary. Possible answers for -tion could be:

- hospitalization → the result of being in the hospital
- discontinuation → the result of discontinuing something

Answers will vary. Possible answers for -ous could be:

- joyous → full of joy
- ridiculous → full of ridicule

SAME THING, DIFFERENT WORD:

1. dangerous
2. chronological
3. government
4. discretion
5. communication

LESSON 3

OPPOSING VIEWS:

1. verdict
2. exaggerated
3. invest
4. accommodate
5. strategy

CATEGORICALLY THINKING:

- strategy
- verdict
- invest
- exaggerate
- accommodate

LESSON 4

KEEP IT CLOZE:

1. Answers will vary. Possible answers could be: Latin, French, our ancestors.
2. calculated
3. Answers will vary. Possible answers could be: my dad starts dancing at a friend's house, my mom starts singing.
4. Answers will vary. Possible answers could be: standing up for others, picking up garbage, saving lives as a lifeguard.
5. paraphrasing

CATEGORICALLY THINKING:

- origin
- embarrass

- calculate
- paraphrased
- heroic

LESSON 5

ASK AND ANSWERED:
Answers will vary.

SAME THING, DIFFERENT WORD:

1. know
2. source
3. humor
4. familiar
5. benefit

LESSON 6

DIGGING FOR ROOTS:
Answers will vary. Possible answers for dis- could be:

- disagree → the opposite of agree
- disobey → the opposite of obey

Add -ion

- vacate → vacation
- discuss → discussion
- meditate → meditation
- explode → explosion

OPPOSING VIEWS:

1. dimension
2. encourage
3. tentative
4. dissatisfied
5. maximum

LESSON 7

KEEP IT CLOZE:
1. hostile
2. Answers will vary. Possible answers could be: jewelry, valuables, money, sentimental items
3. Answers will vary. Possible answers could be: Sweden, New Zealand, Canada, Ireland, the United States
4. museums
5. forecast

ASK AND ANSWERED:
Answers will vary.

LESSON 8

DIGGING FOR ROOTS:
Answers will vary. Possible answer for -ty could be:
- responsibility → denotes being responsible

Answers will vary. Possible answer for grad- could be:
- graduation → stepping out of school

SAME THING, DIFFERENT WORD:
1. gradually
2. extensive
3. guilty
4. equation
5. generous

LESSON 9

OPPOSING VIEWS:
1. citizen
2. abolish
3. persuade
4. behavior
5. analyze

CATEGORICALLY THINKING:
- behavior
- analyze
- persuade
- abolish
- citizen

LESSON 10

KEEP IT CLOZE:
1. approximate
2. Answers will vary. Possible answers could be: flies, krill, bees
3. Answers will vary. Possible answers could be: voice, kindness, smile
4. Answers will vary. Possible answers could be: learning another language, skiing, riding a bike
5. exhausting

CATEGORICALLY THINKING:
- swarm
- exhausted
- approximately
- accomplish
- quality

LESSON 11

ASK AND ANSWERED:
Answers will vary.

OPPOSING VIEWS:
1. ceases
2. arid
3. courage
4. accumulate
5. remain

LESSON 12

DIGGING FOR ROOTS:
Answers will vary. Possible answers for anim could be:
- animal → a living organism
- animosity → feeling dislike or hate

Answers will vary. Possible answers for co-, com-, and con- could be:
- communication → to discuss something together
- complementary → combining to enhance the qualities of one another
- constitutional → rules that work together to create principles for governing a state
- coauthor → a writer that works with another writer

OPPOSING VIEWS:
1. declared
2. compose
3. obedient
4. unanimous
5. opposed

LESSON 13

KEEP IT CLOZE:
1. artifacts
2. Answers will vary. Possible answers could be: 100 pounds, 700 pounds, 80 pounds
3. Answers will vary. Possible answers could be: the solar system, what pigs eat, how dogs learn
4. manipulate
5. ancient

ASK AND ANSWERED:
Answers will vary.

LESSON 14

DIGGING FOR ROOTS:
Answers will vary. Possible answers for *-ent* could be:
- excellent → the process of excelling
- obedient → the process of obeying

SAME THING, DIFFERENT WORD:
1. impatient
2. superior
3. vertical
4. consistently
5. massive

LESSON 15

OPPOSING VIEWS:
1. mention
2. rhythm
3. drastic
4. service
5. consequence

CATEGORICALLY THINKING:
- rhythm
- service
- consequence
- drastic
- mention

LESSON 16

KEEP IT CLOZE:
1. Answers will vary. Possible answers could be: J. K. Rowling, Cynthia Rylant, Rick Riordan
2. squeezes
3. moreover
4. contribute
5. quest

CATEGORICALLY THINKING:
- contribute
- squeeze

- quest
- narrate
- moreover

LESSON 17

ASK AND ANSWERED:
Answers will vary.

SAME THING, DIFFERENT WORD:
1. variable
2. quote
3. adapt
4. peculiar
5. tension

LESSON 18

DIGGING FOR ROOTS:
Answers will vary. Possible answers for *vac* could be:
- vacation → a period of leisure spent away from home or traveling
- vacuum → a space entirely devoid of matter
- vacant → empty

Answers will vary. Possible answers for *trans* could be:
- translucent → allowing light to pass through
- transfix → render motionless because of surprise
- transformation → the act of changing in shape or appearance
- transitory → lasting a very short time

OPPOSING VIEWS:
1. vacate
2. monotonous
3. unruly
4. transport
5. transferred

LESSON 19

KEEP IT CLOZE:
1. specific
2. Answers will vary. Possible answers could be: white dress, jeans, gym shoes
3. Answers will vary. Possible answers could be: a kind personality, a nice smile, the ability to negotiate
4. adequate
5. Answers will vary. Possible answers could be: tired, uninformed, hungry

ASK AND ANSWERED:
Answers will vary.

LESSON 20

DIGGING FOR ROOTS:
Answers will vary. Possible answers for *-tion* could be:
- differentiation → where something is different
- experimentation → where something is experimented
- situation → where something is situated

Answers will vary. Possible answers for *sub-* could be:
- subconscious → physical activity below the level of awareness
- subliminal → information that is below the threshold of your perception
- subordinate → an assistant under the control of someone else

SAME THING, DIFFERENT WORD:
1. outstanding
2. foundation
3. selection

4. substitute
5. treacherous

LESSON 21

OPPOSING VIEWS:
1. business
2. insist
3. revolt
4. anguish
5. gist

CATEGORICALLY THINKING:
- anguish
- revolt
- gist
- insist
- business

LESSON 22

KEEP IT CLOZE:
1. Answers will vary. Possible answers could be: 4 foot 4 inches, 5 feet tall
2. Answers will vary. Possible answers could be: cats, fish, birds
3. cough
4. factor
5. Answers will vary. Possible answers could be: miserable, sad, horrified

CATEGORICALLY THINKING:
- viewpoint
- factor
- toxic
- height
- cough

LESSON 23

ASK AND ANSWERED:
Answers will vary.

SAME THING, DIFFERENT WORD:
1. lofty
2. conserve
3. knack
4. philosophy
5. negotiate

LESSON 24

DIGGING FOR ROOTS:
Answers will vary. Possible answers for *-sion* could be:
- conclusion → the result of an ending
- invasion → the result of someone invading

Answers will vary. Possible answers for *-ive* could be:
- supportive → to give support
- narrative → to narrate

OPPOSING VIEWS:
1. ferocious
2. objective
3. influence
4. expression
5. effective

LESSON 25

KEEP IT CLOZE:
1. Answers will vary. Possible answers could be: French fries, pizza, candy
2. alarming
3. Answers will vary. Possible answers could be: neon yellow, hot pink, bright orange
4. thesis
5. pleasant

ASK AND ANSWERED:
Answers will vary.

LESSON 26

DIGGING FOR ROOTS:
Answers will vary. Possible answers for *-ward* could be:
- eastward → moving East
- straightforward → straight to the point

Answers will vary. Possible answers for *pre-* could be:
- president → leader who sits before all others
- precaution → being cautious beforehand

SAME THING, DIFFERENT WORD:
1. backward
2. predict
3. ridiculous
4. awkward
5. balanced

LESSON 27

OPPOSING VIEWS:
1. catastrophe
2. trembling
3. adjacent
4. solution
5. scarce

CATEGORICALLY THINKING:
- adjacent
- scarce
- catastrophe
- trembling
- solution

LESSON 28

KEEP IT CLOZE:
1. deconstruct
2. capacity
3. Answers will vary. Possible answers could be: hip hop, the piano, knitting

4. retrieve
5. extend

CATEGORICALLY THINKING:
- retrieve
- devote
- extended
- capacity
- deconstruct

LESSON 29

ASK AND ANSWERED:
Answers will vary.

SAME THING, DIFFERENT WORD:
1. suspense
2. similar
3. immigrate
4. announce
5. history

LESSON 30

DIGGING FOR ROOTS:
Answers will vary. Possible answers for *con-* could be:
- concurrently → overlapping in duration
- conformity → coming together with accepted standards, rules, or norms
- congregate → come together, usually for a purpose

OPPOSING VIEWS:
1. congruent
2. hypothesis
3. civilization
4. conclusion
5. confident

LESSON 31

KEEP IT CLOZE:
1. numb
2. daughter

3. Answers will vary. Possible answers could be: garlic bread, sour candy, doughnuts
4. Answers will vary. Possible answers could be: new playground, new classrooms, cafeteria
5. evaluate

ASK AND ANSWERED:
Answers will vary.

LESSON 32

DIGGING FOR ROOTS:
Answers will vary. Possible answers for *-ible* could be:
- audible → able to hear
- reversible → able to be reversed
- digestible → able to be digested

SAME THING, DIFFERENT WORD:
1. ambitions
2. essential
3. illegible
4. oblivious
5. anxious

LESSON 33

OPPOSING VIEWS:
1. violate
2. priority
3. allegiance
4. diminish
5. require

CATEGORICALLY THINKING:
- diminish
- allegiance
- require
- violate
- priority

LESSON 34

KEEP IT CLOZE:
1. Answers will vary. Possible answers could be: biting my nails, procrastinating, gossiping
2. tangible
3. Answers will vary. Possible answers could be: my mom, my friend, my brother
4. elaborate
5. repetition

CATEGORICALLY THINKING:
- elaborate
- repetition
- avoid
- tangible
- ally

LESSON 35

ASK AND ANSWERED:
Answers will vary.

SAME THING, DIFFERENT WORD:
1. ample
2. response
3. unique
4. soothe
5. anticipate

LESSON 36

DIGGING FOR ROOTS:
Answers will vary. Possible answers for *-al* could be:
- optional → having options
- emotional → having emotions

OPPOSING VIEWS:
1. horizontal
2. apprehensive
3. logical
4. proceed
5. frequent

FURTHER RESOURCES

Books! Reading is the one of the best ways to grow a learner's vocabulary. Read together, visit the library, and make books fun in order to grow excitement around reading.

Middle School Vocabulary Words and Word Work by Kelly Anne of Apple Slices LLC. This series provides vocabulary words, worksheets, and assessments for young learners (available on Teachers Pay Teachers).

"The Importance of Teaching Your Students and Children Vocabulary | 4 Ways to Teach Vocabulary at Home and in the Classroom." Blog post by Kelly Anne found at AppleSlicesLLC.com.

Flocabulary.com: A great resource that brings vocabulary to life using videos, online learning, and songs.

Be sure to look into online games and apps that also help children learn new vocabulary.

ACKNOWLEDGMENTS

As a work-from-home mom, there is no way I could have written this book without the help of some important people in my life. From my husband, Jamie, who was always overwhelmingly supportive, willing to think of fun sentences, and able take over playing with our son, Lachlan, so that I could write; to my parents, Pam and Greg, and in-laws, Jody and Jim, who would come into town during the busiest season and pitch in wherever they were needed; to my teacher friends, who always supported me and answered all of my crazy questions about making vocabulary fun.

Moreover, it would never be possible without the help of local friends and family who showed up when times were tight. Thank you, Matt F., Kelci, Matt D., Brianne, Brian, and Brooke. I am so grateful to have a support system that loves and supports all of my endeavors.

ABOUT THE AUTHOR

Kelly Anne McLellan graduated with a degree in elementary education from the University of South Carolina. She has been a teacher since 2010, and has taught students in Colorado, South Carolina, and Spain, in addition to her many online students from around the world. During the early days of her teaching career, she discovered that she really enjoys helping students fall in love with reading and writing, which still influences every aspect of her work. Kelly Anne welcomed her first son in late 2018. As a mom, most of her days are spent chasing after her son and sneaking in time to create writing curriculum for educators when she can. She lives in Wilmington, North Carolina, with her family.